Corfu

by Des Hannigan

Des Hannigan is an experienced travel writer and photographer who has produced several guidebooks as well as books about ancient tracks and historic landscapes. He has written, and contributed to, a number of AA publications. When not travelling and researching, he lives and works in the far west of Cornwall.

Above: *friendship across the generations on Corfu*

AA Publishing

Written by Des Hannigan

First published 1999
Reprinted Aug and Nov 1999; Apr 2000
Reprinted 2001. Information verified and
updated. Reprinted Jun 2001
Reprinted May 2002
This edition 2003. Reprinted 2004

Published by AA Publishing, a trading name of
Automobile Association Developments Limited,
whose registered office is Millstream,
Maidenhead Road, Windsor, Berkshire SL4 5GD.
Registered number 1878835.

Above: *Corfu Town by
night*

A CIP catalogue record for this book is available
from the British Library.

Find out more about
AA Publishing and the
wide range of services
the AA provides by
visiting our website at
www.theAA.com

A02006

Colour separation: Pace Colour, Southampton
Printed and bound in Italy by Printer Trento S.r.l.

Contents

About this Book

This book is divided into five sections to cover the most important aspects of your visit to Corfu.

Viewing Corfu pages 5–14
An introduction to Corfu by the author.
   Corfu's Features
   Essence of Corfu
   The Shaping of Corfu
   Peace and Quiet
   Corfu's Famous

Top Ten pages 15–26
The author's choice of the Top Ten places to see in Corfu, listed in alphabetical order, each with practical information.

What to See pages 27–90
The five main areas of Corfu, each with its own brief introduction and an alphabetical listing of the main attractions.
   Practical information
   Snippets of 'Did you know…' information
   3 suggested walks
   4 suggested tours
   3 features

Where To... pages 91–116
Detailed listings of the best places to eat, stay, shop, take the children and be entertained.

Practical Matters pages 117–24
A highly visual section containing essential travel information.

Maps
All map references are to the individual maps found in the What to See section of this guide.
For example, Kanóni has the reference ➕ 28B3 – indicating the page on which the map is located and the grid square in which the resort is to be found. A list of the maps that have been used in this travel guide can be found in the index.

Greek Place-names
Romanised spellings of Greek names can vary. In place-name headings and in the index, this book uses transliterations which follow a recognised convention and which correspond to AA maps. More familiar Anglicised spellings (given in brackets in the headings) are sometimes used in the text.

Prices
Where appropriate, an indication of the cost of an establishment is given by € signs:
€€€ denotes higher prices, €€ denotes average prices, while € denotes lower charges.

Star Ratings
Most of the places described in this book have been given a separate rating:
✪✪✪   Do not miss
✪✪   Highly recommended
✪   Worth seeing

Viewing Corfu

Above: *a glorious sunset view from Pélekas*
Right: *there is always time to relax in Greece*

Des Hannigan's Corfu

Names Old and New

The modern name of Corfu is said to derive from the Greek word *koryphai*, meaning 'summit' or 'twin peaks', a reference to the hills of the Old Fortress of Corfu Town. The older name for the island, Corcyra, or Kérkyra in modern Greek, is said to have been adopted in honour of the mythological nymph, Kérkura, who was abducted by Poseidon and brought to the island. In ancient times Corfu was known as Drepane, the word for 'sickle', a reference to the island's curved and elongated shape.

Romantic Legend

Corfu has been claimed as being the idyllic Scheria – 'like a shield laid on the misty sea', wrote Homer – the island of the Phaeacians, where the shipwrecked Odysseus was discovered by Nausicaa, daughter of King Alcinous. Several places on Corfu's coastline lay claim to the spot where Odysseus was washed ashore, but the lovely bay at Érmones on the west coast is the favoured site.

Corfu is still the 'Garden Isle' of Greece. It delights with its natural beauty, its glorious beaches, its good food and its choice of nightlife. Yet Corfu's rich heritage adds much more to the holiday experience, with its dramatic history as a Mediterranean paradise shaped by Byzantine, Roman and Venetian cultures, and by later French and British influences; a crossroads of East and West that has remained essentially Greek at heart.

Many things define the essential Corfu. There is, of course, the exquisite heat of summer and the crystal-clear sea. But Corfu is an all-year-round experience – the fragrance of orange blossom in winter; the brilliant colours of wild flowers in spring and again in autumn; the excitement of a festival in Corfu Town or in outlying villages; the soft chimes of sheep bells in mountain meadows; the hissing of cicadas in the heat; and the warm scent of pine. Then there are the early mornings on the western beaches when the coolness of the night lingers on the sea air; hushed afternoons in remote mountain villages; pleasant evening strolls through Corfu Town; the sweetness of a summer's dusk after a long day of sea and sun; feasts of good traditional Greek food and wine in village tavernas; sunset drinks above the glittering Mediterranean.

Above all, there is the charm of the Corfiots, the people of the island, whose vibrant and colourful history has produced a friendly, cosmopolitan society in which the visitor is always made to feel at home.

Night falls on the Old Fortress of Corfu Town

Corfu's Features

Geography

• Position: Corfu is the most northerly of the Ionian Islands. The southeast coast lies about 10km from mainland Greece, the northeast about 2km from Albania.
• Area: 592sq km.
• Highest point: Mount Pandokrator, at 906m.
• Length, north to south: 60km.
• Width, east to west: 4km to 30km. Length of coastline: 217km.
• Population: 110,000 approximately, of which about 35,000 live in Corfu Town.

Climate

• Corfu has a higher average rainfall than the rest of Greece. The highest monthly rainfall is in December, with 240mm. The summer months are almost entirely dry.
• Average daily sunshine, May–September: 10 hours.
• Average temperature, July–August: 32°C.
• Average temperature, December–January: 15°C.

Economic Factors

About 65 per cent of Corfu's land is under cultivation. Of this, 55 per cent is devoted to olive trees, of which there are an estimated 3.5 million. The rest of the cultivated area is used for vineyards, citrus fruit, vegetables and grazing. About one million tourists visit Corfu annually and an estimated third of Corfu's working population is involved in tourism and its related industries.

Harvesting Olives

Fallen olives were once painstakingly collected by hand. Now, nets are spread beneath the trees to make harvesting less labour intensive, but the work is still extremely hard. The Corfu olive, introduced by the Venetians, is used mainly to produce oil, rather than for eating as a fruit. Although some locals eat raw olives like grapes, visitors are advised not to: the experience is bitter.

Essence of Corfu

Below: *a relaxed view from Kanóni's Viewpoint Café*
Inset: *Corfu Town's Old Philharmonic brass band leads a religious procession*

To enjoy all the attractions of Corfu in the space of a holiday visit is a challenge, especially when simply lying on a glorious beach is so relaxing. Understandably, Corfu's superb resorts are often the main attraction and the main base for visitors. But hidden Corfu, the astonishing variety of the island's countryside, the charm and colour of Venetian Corfu Town, the timeless appeal of country villages – none of these should be missed. Relax, soak up the sun, but plan adventures and set aside days for exploring, too. Sample as much as you can; take away a mix of memories.

THE **10** ESSENTIALS

Everything about Corfu is fascinating to the visitor, but there are certain places and certain experiences that should not be missed. Below are some of the essentials:

• **Explore Corfu Town** (▶ 30). Absorb the hectic buzz of modern San Rocco Square, then stroll northeast along Georgiou Theotoki and Voulgareos streets, with side steps into the shaded alleyways of the Old Town, before bursting out into the sunshine and open space of the Spianáda (Esplanade).

• **Walk along a track** through peaceful olive groves, on the hills, or above the sea.

• **Eat at a top-quality** village or beach taverna where good Greek food is served, such as Stamatis at Virós, or Toula's at Agni. Be talkative, be lively. Indulge yourself.

• **Take a boat trip** round the coast, or out to the Diapondía Islands, or south to Paxoí. A leisurely view from the sea increases familiarity with Corfu.

• **Visit one of Corfu's** inland villages, such as Doukádes, Ágios Matthéos, Lefkímmi, or Sinarádes. Wander freely, but discreetly, into authentic Corfu.

• **Swim...**and swim again...and again...and again...

• **Visit at least some** of Corfu Town's historic, religious and cultural sites.

• **Live a little nightlife**, depending on your taste. Try the sound and light shows in the Old Citadel, a Greek evening in a taverna, a blitz of beat at any of the resort clubs or on the disco strip on Eth Antistasseos on the coast road to the northwest of Corfu Town.

• **Visit Paleokastritsa** for its astonishing coastal and mountain landscape, its small but delightful beaches, its

absorbing monastery, and the drama of the nearby hilltop ruin of Angelókastro.

• **Climb Mount Pandokrator** or Mount Ágios Matthéos, but go as early in the day as possible.

Below: *Kassiópi fishing boat*
Inset: *nightlife in Cofu*
Bottom: *beach fun at Glyfáda*

9

The Shaping of Corfu

8000 BC
Corfu becomes an island when sea levels rise at the end of the Ice Ages.

6000 BC
The island is settled by neolithic hunter-gatherers.

3000–1000 BC
Several Bronze Age settlements are established throughout Corfu.

750 BC
Eretrians colonise the Kanóni Peninsula. They may have named their settlement Corcyra (Kérkyra) after the mythological goddess Kérkura.

734 BC
Political refugees from Corinth supplant the Eretrians and establish a thriving colony, which remains at odds with Corinth.

433 BC
A major sea battle between Corcyra and Corinth ends in stalemate, but reflects Corcyra's maritime strength.

303 BC–229 BC
Corcyra is invaded at various times by adventurers from Syracuse, by later Macedonian kings, and finally by Illyrian pirates, who prey on Roman ships.

229 BC
Islanders, in agreement with the Illyrian overlord of Corcyra, offer allegiance to Rome. Corcyra becomes a Roman colony, the first in Greece, but retains control of its own law-making and commerce.

AD 70
Christian influence is brought to the island

by Saints Jason and Sosipater (➤ 33).

395
Corcyra comes under the control of the Byzantine Empire.

550
The island is devastated by Goth invaders, the last in a series of Barbarian and Saracen attacks. The promontory, where the Old Fortress now stands, becomes the nucleus of a fortified town. The name Corfu, from the Greek word *koryphai*, meaning 'summit' or 'twin peaks', first emerges.

1080
Corfu is taken over by the Norman Robert Guiscard, King of Sicily. In 1149 Corfu is recaptured by the Byzantine Emperor Manuel Comnenus.

1206
Capture of Constantinople by the Franks.

1214
Michael I, Despot of Epirus, takes over Corfu. Renewed Byzantine influence underpins the official position of the Greek Church.

Robert Guiscard, King of Sicily, ruled over Corfu in 1080

An icon depicting incidents in the life of St Spyrídon

1570s
Building of the New Fortress.

1716
Second major Turkish siege is repulsed.

1797
Corfu and the other Ionian Islands are captured by the French.

1814
Corfu becomes part of the United States of the Ionian Islands under British Protection.

1864
On 21 May, Corfu becomes part of united Greece, whose first Governor is the Corfu-born politician Ioannis Kapodistrias (John Capodistrias).

1940–44
Corfu Town bombed by the Italians, and later by the Germans.

1960s
Development of mass tourism.

1994
Corfu hosts the EC summit.

2002
Greece adopts the euro as its currency.

1267
The Neapolitan House of Anjou gains control of Corfu.

1386
Corfu offers allegiance to Venetians, who rule the island for four centuries on a mercantile and feudal basis. Orthodox religion and Greek customs and culture survive.

1456
The body of St Spyrídon is brought to Corfu from Constantinople.

1537
First major siege by the Turks, who ravage the island but fail to take the Old Fortress and Angelókastro. They withdraw with about 15,000 prisoners.

1565
Venetians order the uprooting of vineyards and a widespread planting of olive trees, a scheme finally achieved only by offering farmers handsome payment for every 100 trees planted.

Peace & Quiet

Towns and Villages
Peace and quiet is not only a rural luxury. In busy, bustling Corfu Town there are oases of calm, such as the larger Orthodox churches that are open to the public, the various museums, and the British Cemetery (➤ 33). And, in mountain villages, a more relaxed, more serene attitude is the norm.

The view from the summit of Mount Pandokrator looking towards distant Albania

The lushness of Corfu's famous olive groves is a pleasing contrast to the cobalt blue of the Mediterranean. It is this wealth of woodland that provides the island's havens of peace and quiet, areas where the beach-weary visitor can explore and find cool shade from the sun. On the higher ground of the mountains, and along the undeveloped coast, there are other opportunities to escape from the crowds.

Walking*

The best walking areas are on the more remote northeast and west coasts, and on the high ground of Mount Pandokrator, Mount Ágios Matthéos and Mount Ágios Déka. However, by walking inland through olive groves, peace and quiet can also be found within a few metres of busy resorts. Of interest to any walking enthusiast is the Corfu Trail, a 200km fully-marked walk crossing the whole island. The route meanders through diverse landscapes, linking beauty spots, beaches, picturesque villages, monuments and monasteries. The entire walk can be done in 8–12 days, alternatively you can pick out sections, as detailed in the guide book (➤ 13) or on the website (www.corfutrail.com).

Cycling

Hire bikes can be used for the multitude of off-road tracks on the island. The least hilly areas are in the south, round Límni Korissión and Lefkímmi, in the western Rópa Valley area, and in the north, round coastal Sidári, Róda and Acharávi. But, anywhere on the island, you should be prepared for rough surfaces, pot-holes and for some steep climbs.

Wildlife

Corfu has over 400 species of wild plant, most of which bloom during spring and early summer, while autumn sees another flowering of certain species. Masses of daisies appear early, followed by pink geraniums, marigolds, irises, poppies and grape hyacinths, among many others. On the higher ground of the mountains, blue anemones and bell-headed fritillaries light up the landscape, while the limestone rocks are clothed in purple-pink soapwort. Over 30 species of orchid grow on Corfu, including the bee orchid, Jersey orchid, man orchid, tongue orchid and monkey orchid.

Migrant birds pass through Corfu in vast numbers in spring and autumn. Species include warblers, flycatchers, whitethroats, and the jackdaw-sized blue roller. Summer residents include swallows, sand martins and bee-eaters.

A cocktail of fragrances from Corfu's flowers and shrubs attracts numerous butterflies, such as the yellow-orange cleopatra, the chocolate-brown Camberwell beauty, and the long-tailed blue.

Reptiles include the harmless four-lined snake, which can grow to over a metre in length. Two venomous species are the Lataste's, or horn viper, recognised by its distinctive horned nose, and the Montpellier snake, grey, brown or olive in colour and with prominent ridges over the eyes. Such snakes will instinctively avoid you. The most avid 'biters' on Corfu are midsummer horse-flies.

* The excellent *Green Map* of Corfu details roads, dirt tracks and trails. Highly recommended guides are *The Second Book of Corfu Walks: The Road to Old Corfu*, *In the Footsteps of Lawrence Durrell and Gerald Durrell in Corfu* and *The Companion Guide to the Corfu Trail*, all by Hilary Whitton Paipeti.

Below: *the Hottentot fig (Mesembryanthemum) adds colour to Corfu's coast*
Bottom: *butterflies settle like jewels on Corfu's greenery*

Corfu's Famous

Island Talent

Corfu-based painters of Cretan origin, such as Emmanuel Tzanes (1610–90) and Michael Damaskinos (1530–92), have produced some of the finest icon paintings of Greece. Modern Corfiot painters include Nikos Venturas (1899–1990) and Papa Aglaia (1904–84). Corfu has also inspired several famous British exiles, including the painter and writer Edward Lear (1812–88) and the writers Gerald and Lawrence Durrell.

St Spyrídon

St Spyrídon (AD 270–*c*348) is the patron saint of Corfu and a focus of strong devotion on the island where he is known simply as 'The Saint'. Spyrídon was a Cypriot bishop, said to have performed numerous miracles. During the 7th century, the saint's revered remains were transferred from Cyprus to Constantinople, but, on the fall of the city in 1453, his body was brought, eventually, to Corfu by an itinerant priest. The remains lie in the Church of St Spyrídon (▶ 17). St Spyrídon is associated with several miraculous events which saved the island from plague, famine and Turkish siege and these are celebrated with solemn, but colourful, processions in which his remains are carried through Corfu Town.

Ioannis Kapodistrias (John Capodistrias)

Count John Capodistrias (1776–1831) was a celebrated Corfiot who, in 1827, became the first President of Independent Greece. In 1831 his career was cut short, however, when he was assassinated at Náfplio in the Peloponnese by critics of his political programme.

Born in Corfu in 1776, Capodistrias practised as a doctor, and then entered island politics. During the French occupation of Corfu he left the island and joined the Russian foreign service. In 1822 he retired and devoted himself to the cause of Greek independence.

Capodistrias is buried in Moní Platytéras (the Monastery of Platitéra) in Corfu Town. A small museum in Evropoúli, to the west of the town, celebrates his life.

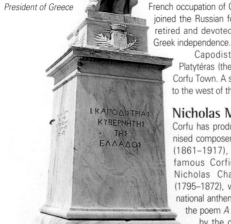

Statue of Ioannis Kapodistrias, native of Corfu and first President of Greece

Nicholas Mantzaros

Corfu has produced internationally recognised composers such as Spiros Samaras (1861–1917), but probably the most famous Corfiot musical celebrity is Nicholas Chalikiopoulos Mantzaros (1795–1872), who composed the Greek national anthem as an accompaniment to the poem *A Hymn to Freedom*, written by the celebrated poet Dionysios Solomos. Mantzaros devoted much of his later life to teaching and, at times, to financing young Corfiot students.

Top Ten

Above: *the islands of Vlachérna and
Pontikonísi, Kanóni*
Right: *the 'Dying Achilles' in
the Achilleion Palace
gardens*

1
Achilleío
(Achilleion Palace)

*Corfu's famous Achilleion Palace is a delightful
expression of 19th-century classicism and
indulgence, set within beautiful surroundings.*

*Thie richly elegant
entrance hall of the
Achilleion Palace*

 28B3

✉ Gastoúri village.
Signposted from Corfu
Town and from the
coast road north of
Benítses

☎ (06610) 56245

🕐 Daily 8–6

🍴 Cafés (€€) near entrance

🚌 Blue bus 10 from San
Rocco Square, Corfu
Town

♿ Few

💶 Moderate

↔ Benítses (➤ 64)

❓ Roadside parking only

The Achilleion, a fascinating relic of 19th-century grand
design, stands on tree-clad heights above the east coast
resort of Benítses, adjacent to the village of Gastoúri. It
was conceived by the Empress Elizabeth of Austria as a
tribute to her spiritual hero Achilles, and the result is a
splendid confection of colonnades and stucco work based
on the classical elegance of Pompeii, the whole crowded
with statues, paintings and 19th-century furnishings.

Six years after the palace was completed in 1892, the
Empress was killed by an assassin on the quayside of Lake
Geneva. In 1908 the palace was bought by Kaiser Wilhelm
II, who added his own grandiose touches before leaving
Corfu in 1914 for more pressing engagements – he never
returned. Eventually taken over by the Greek state, the
Achilleion lay unused until it was converted into a casino in
1963. Today, the casino is part of the Corfu Holiday Palace,
and the Achilleion is a serious cultural attraction.

On view is the ornately decorated entrance hall, the
Empress's chapel, and ground-floor reception rooms
containing furnishings and memorabilia of the Empress
and the Kaiser. In the terraced gardens, beneath the shade
of cypresses and palm trees, are numerous statues
including the Empress's favourite, the sentimental 'Dying
Achilles', and the Kaiser's contribution, an outrageously
monumental 'Achilles Triumphant'.

2

Ágios Spyrídonas
(Church of St Spyrídon)

Ágios Spyrídonas is the most famous church in Corfu. Built in 1590 to house the sacred relics of St Spyrídon, it is a place of pilgrimage to this day.

The tall, red-domed bell-tower of Ágios Spyrídonas, reminiscent of the tower of San Giorgio dei Greci in Venice, is a landmark of central Corfu Town. Plain outside walls hide a lavish interior: there is a superb iconostasis (a screen of white Cycladian marble); silver thuribles and candelabra crowd the basilica; and a wealth of paintings and icons decorate the walls.

In spite of the steady procession of the faithful – and the merely curious – which passes across the pink-and-white flagstones and through the doors to either side, there is a subdued atmosphere inside the church. Candles still flicker in the gloom 'like yellow crocuses', as vividly described by Gerald Durrell in his reminiscences of a Corfu childhood. Young and old, the plain and the fashionable pay homage to St Spyrídon.

The real focus of the church, however, is the ornate casket containing the mummified remains of the saint. These are exposed annually on 12 December (St Spyrídon's Day), at Easter, and on 11 August. The saint's feet are clad in embroidered slippers, which devotees claim become worn because of Spyrídon's frequent night-time wanderings round the Old Town. The casket, silver-coated and bearing 12 enamel medallions, is situated to the right of the altar, within a separate chapel, beneath lamps and votive offerings from which dangle tiny silver ships and other motifs. Only a few steps take you from the dazzling sunshine of the outside world into this intense focus of Greek Orthodoxy.

An icon of the Virgin and Child (1707) in the sanctuary of Ágios Spyrídonas

✚ 32B5

✉ Ayiou Spiridonas Street, Corfu Town. Can also be reached from Plateía Iroon Kypriakou Agonos, known also as St Spyrídon's Square

🕐 Daily 9–2. Casual visits during services are best avoided

🍴 Café Plakada (€€) in St Spyrídon's Square

♿ Good (best access is from Ayiou Spiridonas Street)

✋ Free, donations welcome

❓ Sober clothing should be worn

3
Angelókastro

✚ 28A5

✉ Krini. Just west of
Makrádes (follow the
signs) and 28km from
Corfu Town

🕐 Open access

🍴 Sunset Taverna (€€) on
the approach to Krini

🚌 Green bus from
Avramiou Street, Corfu
Town–Makrádes

♿ None

💰 Cheap

↔ Paleokastritsa (► 24)

❓ Small car park below
the fortress. Take care
near the unprotected
cliff edges

*The fortress of
Angelókastro has a
spectacular setting: richly
wooded hill slopes on
three sides and the sea
on the fourth*

*The 12th-century ruin of the Byzantine fortress of
Angelókastro occupies a spectacular rocky hill top on
the west coast.*

Angelókastro is one of the finest historic sites on Corfu.
Fortified in the 12th century, it may later have been named
after the Byzantine family of Angeloi Comneni, which ruled
Corfu from 1214 until 1267. The fortress played a key role
in the successful defence of the island for hundreds of
years, as from it a watch could be kept on the vulnerable
west coast and signals exchanged with Corfu Town.
Angelókastro's greatest test came when several thousand
islanders withstood sieges by Turkish invaders in 1537,
1571 and 1716. Military use of Angelókastro ended in the
19th century during the British Protectorate.

The ruins of the fortress stand on top of a rocky
pinnacle whose seaward cliffs drop 300m into the sea.
During the spring, wild roses and orchids speckle the
steep slopes. Cobbled steps wind steeply from a convenient car park to a narrow entrance into the inner keep,
above which is the upper keep, crowned by the tiny
Church of the Archangels Michael and Gabriel, another
possible source of Angelókastro's name. In front of the
church are seven grave moulds cut into the rock.

Just east of the summit, and at a lower level, are the
remains of underground water cisterns. In the lower keep,
on the far left of the entrance, is a remarkable hermitage –
a rocky cave that was converted into a chapel to St Kyriaki
in the late 18th century. Wall-paintings of the Virgin and
Christ survive.

4

Campiello:
Old Corfu Town

*The old part of Corfu Town is known as
Campiello. It lies behind the seafront between the
Old and New Fortresses.*

Venetian is the emphatic style of Campiello's buildings and its fascinating maze of narrow streets, the *kandounia*, which spreads between the main thoroughfares; lanes are often linked by stone stairways (*skalinades*), and by vaulted passageways. The original buildings of the medieval town, which developed on the cramped peninsula as a domestic adjunct to the Old Fortress, eventually replacing it as the administrative centre of the island, are long gone. Here, the Venetians built grand Renaissance houses three or four storeys high, which were added to in later centuries to accommodate a growing population whose members were reluctant to move outside the town walls.

Venetian motifs survive on the sometimes crumbling façades of these wonderful old buildings and on the doorcases, or *portonia*, with their distinctive mouldings. Throughout the day the sun weaves an intricate pattern of shifting light on the walls and turns them to burnished gold in the evening. In the narrow, sun-dappled canyons of Campiello, lines of washing hang like banners between the upper windows, and the mottled walls rise cliff-like past railed balconies and stone pediments to a final blue ribbon of sky. Underfoot the ground is smoothly paved, and intriguing courtyards, terraced gardens, ancient churches and shrines appear round every other corner. There are neighbourhood shops, cafés, tavernas, bars and workplaces where Corfiots busy themselves with trade and craft. In the mellow evenings, you may catch the sound of musicians practising in the club rooms of the town's four brass bands.

*A typical narrow street
(kandounia) in Campiello*

 32B5

 Numerous cafés,
tavernas and
restaurants throughout
the Old Town

None. Steps link a
number of alleyways
and streets

5
Kalámi

✈ 28C5

✉ Just off the main coast road, 30km north of Corfu Town

🍴 Pepes (€€)

🚌 Green bus from Avramiou Street, Corfu Town–Kassiópi/Loútses

⛴ Small ferry boats from nearby resorts

♿ None

↔ Kouloúra (➤ 74)

❓ Limited parking

Kalámi lies on Corfu's northeast coast, amid a landscape of quiet bays backed by the tree-clad slopes of Mount Pandokrator.

In the famous White House at Kalámi, the writer Lawrence Durrell lived for a time and there wrote his lyrical book *Prospero's Cell*. Today, Kalámi's idyllic peace and quiet, the 'charms of seclusion' described so vividly by Durrell, are no more. Seen from the north, however, its deep-blue bay caught within a green amphitheatre of olives and cypresses, the village still reflects the quintessential beauty of old Corfu. Unfortunately, the view from the south includes the modern terraced apartments that dominate the west side of the bay – they would benefit from being painted in a Cycladean white rather than their faded purple.

The White House, 'set like a dice on a rock already venerable with the scars of wind and water', stands on the

Lawrence Durrell's Kalámi reflects the classic beauty of Corfu's northeast coast

south side of the bay. It is distinctly English-looking, with its solid, square shape and its broad, hipped roof. Here Durrell and his wife, Nancy, lived what seems to have been a truly idyllic life in the Ionian sun. Their quickest way to Corfu Town was by boat and the Durrells travelled a great deal in their little sailing boat, the *Van Norden*. Their friends were a collection of serene eccentrics. Even the dynamic Henry Miller was persuaded to visit for a time and was captivated by Greece. Today, the White House functions as a taverna with apartments above.

Kalámi has a number of other tavernas, interspersed with villas, the whole softened by groves of orange and lemon trees, olives and cypresses. Although the resort is busy in summer, it is quiet in the evenings. Boats can be hired, and the beach is very safe for children.

6
Kanóni

The resort lies at the southern tip of the Kanóni Peninsula overlooking the two little islands of Vlachérna and Pontikonísi (Mouse Island).

The view of Vlachérna, with its little convent and its solitary cypress tree, and of Pontikonísi, with its thicket of trees and its chapel, is probably the most photographed in the Ionian Islands, an enduring visual symbol of modern Corfu. The sounds accompanying this scenic delight are less soothing: Corfu's airport runway slices across the adjoining lagoon, Chalkiopoúlou, a few hundred metres away. (Youngsters will love plane-spotting).

There is precedent for sound and fury, however. Kanóni is so named from being the site of a gun battery, first established by the French during the British blockade of Corfu from 1810 to 1815. Today, a Russian cannon, installed about 30 years ago to add colour, stands on the viewing terrace by the café and gift shop overlooking Vlachérna and Pontikonísi. Winding steps lead down from the terrace to the little harbour, from where Vlachérna is reached along a causeway. The Convent of the Virgin Mary here has a fine little Venetian belfry. Boats ferry visitors to Pontikonísi and run to and from Corfu Town. The little Byzantine Church of Pandokrator on Pontikonísi, said to date from the 11th or 12th century, has a characteristic octagonal dome and cross vaults, and a three-sided apse. Inside it is sparse and unadorned except for marble wall plaques recording past royal visits. The islet is one of the many candidates for being the ship turned to stone, by a jealous Poseidon, on its return from ferrying Odysseus to Ithaca.

✚ 28B3

✉ At the southernmost tip of the Kanóni Peninsula, 5km south of Corfu Town

🍴 Taverna Pelargos (€€).

🚌 2 Kanóni. Blue bus from San Rocco Square

⛴ Caique ferries to and from Corfu Town

♿ None

↔ Pérama (► 84)

❓ Limited parking by the viewing terrace. Follow parking signs on the approach road and branch right, signed Pontikonísi, to reach the unsurfaced harbourside car park

Vlachérna is linked to the mainland by a causeway, but the most popular way to arrive is by boat

7

Límni Korissión
(Lake Korissión)

Southwest Corfu is low-lying, a gentle foil to the mountainous north. Lake Korissión lies on the scimitar curve of the coast behind the remote Halikounas Beach.

🔲 28B2

✉ On the west coast about 20km south of Corfu Town

🍴 Taverna (€) at north end of lake

↔ Gardíki Castle (► 68)

❓ The north end of the lake is reached by following signposts for Gardíki from a junction about 1km south of Moraïtika. The south end is reached by turning west off the main road to Kávos, at Línia, and following signs for Paralía tou Íssou (Issos Beach)

Lake Korissión is a man-made lagoon of 607ha, created by the Venetians, who constructed a short, reinforced channel from the sea and flooded existing marshlands. It offers a peaceful respite from crowded beaches and the more popular resorts. Inland, the lake is bordered by low hills and, to the north, Mount Ágios Matthéos looms large. Even the ever-present olive relents here, to be replaced by silvery-green juniper and cedar trees that lie scattered along the lake shores and on the headlands, amid thickets of reeds. Flowering plants at Korissión include the spring catchfly, or loose-flowered orchid, with its purple blooms, just one of the dozen or so orchid species that flourish here. Summer sees the blue-green sea holly and various spurges; later in the season, the beautiful white flowers of the sand lily, or sea daffodil, gleam in the dunes.

The lake and its margins provide an ideal winter habitat for birds. Over 120 species have been recorded here, including rare migrants such as the great white egret and the glossy ibis. Overwintering visitors include mallard, shelduck and teal, while waders such as greenshank, avocets and black-winged stilts are often in residence, along with the more common oystercatcher and curlew.

The neck of the channel at the entrance to the lake is blocked with fish traps to control the passage and catching of grey mullet – a rough track runs down the seaward edge of the lake from its northern end to a fish-watcher's hut beside the channel. One of the charms of Lake Korissión is its remoteness, and it has the bonus of a stretch of sandy beach north and south of the channel.

The broad waters of Lake Korissión on Corfu's remote southwest coast

8
Mouseío Archaiologikó
(Archaeological Museum)

*Corfu Town's small, but rewarding,
Archaeological Museum houses some outstanding
relics from the island's ancient past.*

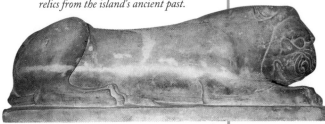

The museum contains one of the finest prehistoric relics in all of Greece, the famous Gorgon pediment recovered from the ruins of the 6th-century BC Temple of Artemis on the Kanóni Peninsula. Though it is not intact, the pediment, 17m long and 3m high, has been restored skilfully. Such monumental antiquity may seem incidental to devoted beach lovers, but the impact of the snake-haired, eye-popping Medusa sheltering her blood offspring, Chrysaor and Pegasus, attended by Zeus and slaughtered Titans and flanked by leopards, is enough to draw breath from the most jaded onlooker. The glaring eyes seem to follow you about the room.

The Gorgon frieze is matched, in the South Hall, by the splendid Lion of Menekrates, a limestone sculpture of the late 7th century BC. Discovered in 1843, it is considered to be one of the finest examples of early Corinthian art, a fluid and life-like creation. Gaze long enough and you begin to suspect that the lion may leap.

Other delights include some excellent tomb monuments, classical pottery and Bronze Age artefacts, and an impressive collection of coins dating from the 6th to 3rd centuries BC. In the North Hall there are some splendid terracotta fittings and artefacts from the ruins of a 7th-century temple found in the grounds of Mon Repos villa (➤ 35).

The finest exhibit here is the left side of a limestone pediment featuring the god Dionysus and a naked youth, well supplied with wine and reclining on a couch. Both are avidly watching a scene on the lost half of the pediment, a tantalising omission for the rest of us.

✚ 32B3

✉ 1 Vraila Armeni Street

☎ (06610) 30680

🕐 Tue–Sun 8:30–2:30

🍴 Cafés and tavernas in nearby San Rocco Square (€) and on the Liston (€€€)

♿ Excellent

✋ Moderate. Free on Sun

Highlights of Corfu's Archaeological Museum: the Lion of Menekrates (above) and the Gorgon pediment (below)

9
Palaiokastrítsa
(Paleokastritsa)

✝ 28A5

✉ On the west coast of Corfu, 25km from Corfu Town

🍴 Numerous tavernas and cafés in resort

🚌 Green bus from Avramiou Street, Corfu Town–Paleokastritsa

⛴ Boat trips to view coastal features, caves and grottos

♿ None

↔ Angelókastro (➤ 18)

The wooded headlands and crescent-shaped bays of Corfu's most celebrated scenic extravaganza have attracted visitors since the early 19th century.

At Paleokastritsa, towering mountains give way reluctantly to the sea, their tree-clad slopes mottled with great cliffs. Here, the landscape has overwhelmed the human element, instead of the other way round. Roads end at Paleokastritsa, giving a real sense of arrival.

Long before the British holidaymaker first picnicked at 'Paleo', the western headland was home to a **monastery** dedicated to the Virgin Mary. The original foundation was 13th-century, but the present complex is mainly 18th-century. A small church lies at the bone-white heart of the monastery, its walls laden with icons in chunky rococo frames; a fine painting of the Last Judgement hangs above

the south doorway. Lemon trees and bougainvillaea soften the hard brilliance outside, and from the garden terrace there is a breathtaking view across the Bay of Liapádes to Cape Ágios Iliodoros and on to distant Cape Plaka. Within the monastery complex is a preserved oil mill and a small museum displaying icons, and a collection of shells and bones from the sea.

The less spiritual delights of Paleokastritsa include the rather cramped, sun-trap beaches of Ágios Spyrídon, which lie to either side of the main car park. The harbour and beaches at Alipo Bay lie beyond the easterly headland of St Nicholas. There are sun-loungers and watersports equipment, and boats can be hired from the harbour. Organised boat trips visit nearby cliff grottos and caves, and the crystal-clear seas round 'Paleo' are especially good for scuba diving.

Monastery

 8–1, 3–8

Café (€€) outside monastery

A small donation appreciated

? Dress appropriately when visiting the monastery

Above: the Venetian bell-tower of the monastery
Left: the turquoise sea and silver sand at Paleokastritsa

25

10
Pantokrátoras
(Mount Pandokrator)

28C5

✉ Dominates the northeast corner of the island, 37km north of Corfu Town

🍴 Café outside monastery gate

✋ Monastery free, small donation welcome

❓ Roadside parking about 1km from the summit near the junction with the track from Néa (New) Períthia, signposted Pyrgí, Róda and Kassiópi

The mountain's vast bulk, and its rolling hinterland of maquis dense with kermes oak, myrtle and wild flowers, creates a persuasive sense of wilderness and open space.

Pandokrator, at 906m a spectacular viewpoint, was known in prehistory as Istone and by the Venetians as Monte San Salvatore. In the 14th century a church dedicated to Christ Pandocrator, 'The Almighty' or 'The All Embracing One', was built on the summit of the mountain and the name was eventually applied to the entire massif. The present buildings are 19th-century replacements of earlier structures. Today, the monastery shares the crowded summit, rather uneasily, with a huge radio mast and various other beacons and aerials. There is a pilgrimage to the monastery on 6 August each year to celebrate the Feast of the Transfiguration.

From the north the approach is by road, through Néa (New) Períthia (► 84) and then by a track to join the summit road. The best approach, however, is from the south through Spartýlas and the village of Strinýlas. Just beyond Strinýlas, bear right at a junction and on to a good road which leads to the summit. The last kilometre, surfaced with ribbed concrete, is extremely tortuous and steep. Parking space at the summit is limited. It may be more practical, and in some ways more fitting, to walk the last section from roadside parking below the summit. Experienced hillwalkers, with proper clothing, footwear and equipment, will find off-road exploration of the mountain rewarding.

Looking towards Mount Pandokrator beyond sentinel cypress trees

What to See

Above: 'Achilles Triumphant' in the Achilleion Palace
Right: dancer in traditional Corfiot dress

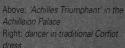

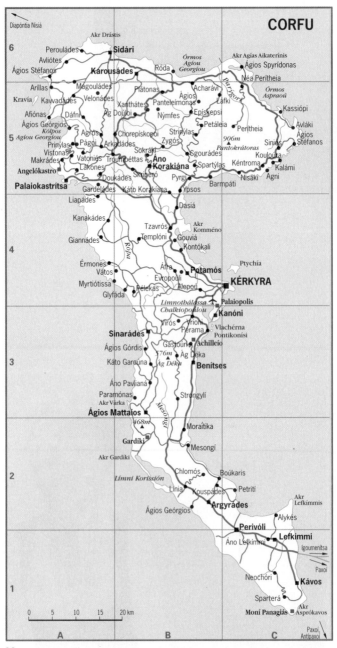

CORFU

Diapóntia Nisiá

Akr Drástis

Perouládes · **Sidári**
Avliótes
Ágios Stéfanos · **Karousádes** · Róda · Órmos Agíou Georgíou · Akr Agías Aikaterínis · **Ágios Spyrídonas**
Néa Perítheia
Arillas · Mégouládes · Plátanos · Acharávi
Kravía · Kavvadádes · Velonádes · Ágios Panteleimonas · Lákki · Órmos Aspraoú
Afiónas · Xanthátes · Épískepsi · Kassiópi
Ágios Geórgios · Dáfni · Ag Doúloi · Nýmfes · Petáleia · Perítheia · Avláki
Kólpos · Agíou Georgíou · Agros · Chorepískopoi · Strinýlas · 906m · Sinies · Ágios Stéfanos
Prímylas · Págoi · Arkadádes · Zygós · Pantokrátoras · Kouloúra
Vístonas · Troúmpettas · Sokráki · **Áno Korakiána** · Sgourádes · Kéntroma · Kalámi
Makrádes · Vatoniés · Lákones · Skriperó · Spartýlas · Agni
Angelókastro · Doukádes · Pyrgi · Nisáki
Palaiokastrítsa · Gardeládes · Káto Korakiána · Ypsos · Barmpáti
Liapádes · Dasiá
Kanakádes
Giannádes · Tzavrós · Akr Komméno
Templóni · Gouviá
Kontókali
Érmones · Áfra · **Potamós** · Ptychía
Vátos · Evropoúli
Myrtiótissa · Pélekas · Alepoú · **KÉRKYRA**
Glyfáda · Limnothálassa Chalkiopoúlou · Palaiópolis
Kanóni
Virós · Vlachérna
Sinarádes · Pérama · Pontikonísi
Ágios Górdis · Gastoúri · **Achilleío**
Káto Garoúna · 576m · Ag Déka
Áno Pavlianá · Ag Déku · **Benítses**
Paramónas · Strongylí
Akr Várka
Ágios Mattaíos · Moraítika
468m
Gardíki · Mesongí
Akr Gardíki · Chlomós · Boúkaris
Límni Korissión · Línia · Kouspádes · Petrití
Akr Lefkímmis
Ágios Geórgios · **Argyrádes**
Alykés
Perivóli · **Lefkímmi**
Áno Lefkímmi · Igoumenítsa
Paxoí
Neochóri · **Kávos**
Spárterá
Moní Panagiás · Akr Asprókavos
Paxoí, Antípaxoi

Róda (river)
Mésongi (river)

0 5 10 15 20 km

A   B   C

Kérkyra (Corfu Town)

The magic of Corfu Town is at its most potent where new and old meet at M Theotoki Square. Here, you step from the bustle of a modern Greek town into the arcaded, smoothly paved streets of medieval Italy, your way signposted by Greek street names, Greek churches, and by a sense of more variety to come.

Soon, you reach the famous Esplanade, its western edge framed by the arcaded Liston, a French tribute to the Parisian rue de Rivoli. At the northern edge of the Esplanade stands the Palace of St Michael and St George, symbol of British neo-classicism. Beyond all this, to the east, Byzantine Greece is represented, in spirit, by the mighty Old Fortress, whose Venetian walls stand on Corinthian foundations. Corfu Town is thus East and West, ancient and modern, classical and exotic – a fascinating, exciting and endearing Mediterranean city, with shops, cafés, restaurants, bars and tavernas to suit all tastes.

> *'The city was Venetian until 1780...nearest the sea, there is the most beautiful esplanade in the world.'*
>
> EDWARD LEAR
> describing Corfu Town in a letter,
> 1848

---●---

Previous page: *watch the world go by in the Old Port area of Corfu Town*

Kérkyra (Corfu Town)

The original settlement of Corfu Town was on the southern tip of the Kanóni Peninsula to the south of the present town, and for centuries this was the commercial and cultural focus of island life. Then, in the 6th century, a more hostile world emerged and the citizens of the town, exhausted from savage barbarian raids, moved to the small twin-peaked peninsula where the Old Fortress now stands. During the centuries that followed, a town developed outside the Fortress, but within its own defensive walls. Later expansion saw Corfu Town spread to the south and west to form an outer shell of suburbs that evolved into the residential and commercial district surrounding San Rocco Square.

The main sights of Corfu Town start at the sea's edge. Enjoy a panoramic view from the airy heights of the Old Fortress; savour the park-like ambience of the Esplanade and the elegance of the Listón. Visit the Church of St Spyrídon and take in the Byzantine Museum or the Municipal Art Gallery, and wander through the maze of alleyways and squares of the Campiello. Stop for coffee, for drinks, and for Greek food. But make sure you take a trip west down the bustling Voulgareos and Georgiou Theotoki streets and into San Rocco Square and the streets that radiate from it. This is where the townspeople live their modern lives, secure in the knowledge that, like you, they can step back into the past at any time.

Corfu Town from the Old Fortress

The fascinating paved alleyways of Corfu Town

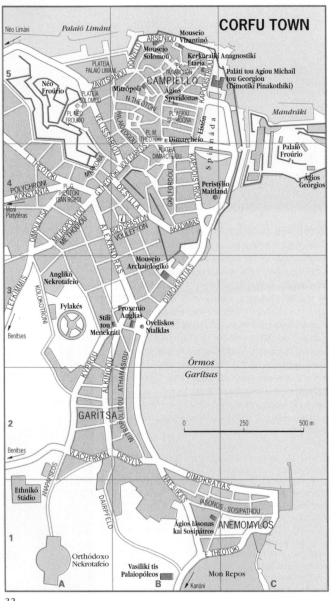

CORFU TOWN

Néo Limáni

Palaió Limáni

ARSENIOU

Mouseío Vizantinó

Mouseío Solomoú

DONZELOT

Kerkuraíkí Anagnostikí Etaría

PLATEÍA PALAIO LIMANI

TAXIARCHON

Paláti tou Agíou Michaíl tou Georgíou (Dimotikí Pinakothíki)

Néo Froúrio

ZAVITSIANOU

CAMPIELLO

PLATEÍA SOLOMOÚ

VELISSARIOU

Mitrópoli

N THEOTÓKI

Ágios Spyrídonas

PL. AGÍOU SPYRÍDONA

PL NÉO FROÚRIO

Mandráki

Listón

PALAIOLOGOU

MYRORI

PL M THEOTÓKI

Dimarcheío

S p i a n á d a

Palaió Froúrio

THEOTÓKI

G. THEOTÓKI

VOULGAREOS

PLATEÍA DIMARCHEÍOU

Ágios Geórgios

POLYCHRONI KONSTANTA

PL. G. THEOTÓKI (SAN ROKO)

DE SYLLA

GKILFORDOU

KAPODISTRIOU

Peristýlio Maitland

Moni Platytéras

DIMOULITSA

MITROPOLITOU METHODOU

ALEXANDRAS

RIZOSPASTON VOULEFTON

AKADIMIAS

LEFKIMMIS

KOLOKOTRONI

Mouseío Archaiologikó

Anglikó Nekrotafeío

DIMOKRATIAS

Fylakés

Proxenío Anglías

Stíli tou Menekráti

Oyelískos Ntalklas

Benitses

KERKYROU

ALKINOOU

MITROPOLITOU ATHANASIOU

Órmos Garítsas

GARÍTSA

0   250   500 m

Benitses

VLACHERNON

DE SYLLA

Ethnikó Stádio

ANAPESEOS

DAIRPFELD

DIMOKRATIAS

NAFSIKAS

IASONOS - SOSIPATROU

Ágios Iásonas kai Sosipátros

ANEMOMYLOS

E. THEOTÓKI

Orthódoxo Nekrotafeío

Vasilikí tis Palaiopóleos

Mon Repos

Kanóni

A   B   C

What to See in Corfu Town

ÁGIOS IÁSONAS KAI SOSIPÁTROS ✪
(CHURCH OF ST JASON AND ST SOSIPATER)

Corfu's sole example of 10th- to early 11th-century Byzantine architecture stands in a rather anonymous corner of Anemomylos, a suburb on the southern edge of Corfu Town. Jason and Sosipater were bishops of Tarsus and Iconium respectively, who brought Christianity to Corfu during the 1st century when the island was under Roman rule. They are said to have been martyred for it. The church is of typical Byzantine design, built in the shape of a cross with a handsome central dome crowning an octagonal drum. Alternate horizontal bands of patterned brick and sandstone blocks decorate the exterior, together with an ornamental frieze. Inside, there are a number of fine icons, and a mix of styles and periods. There is an 18th-century iconostasis, and the plain marble columns that help to support the dome are believed to originate from a classical temple of ancient Palaiopolis (➤ 40).

ÁGIOS SPYRÍDONAS (➤ 17, TOP TEN)

ANGLIKÓ NEKROTAFEÍO (BRITISH CEMETERY) ✪✪

There is nothing gloomy about a visit to this tree-shaded and flower-filled oasis of peace and quiet. More English garden than burial plot, it was established during the period of the British Protectorate and contains the graves of soldiers who died in service during the 19th and 20th centuries. Civilians are buried here, too. The cemetery, under the care of the British War Graves Commission, is lovingly tended by its Corfiot caretaker, George Psailas, who was born in the peaceful little guardian house. Mr Psailas may appear at the mellow chiming of the entrance bell to dispense information in his courteous way.

In spring the cemetery is awash with the colour of shrubs and flowers, most notably a remarkable number of orchids, which are allowed to bloom and seed before grass-cutting begins.

CAMPIELLO (OLD QUARTER) (➤ 19, TOP TEN)

✚ 32B1
✉ Iásonas kai Sosipátros (Jason and Sosipater Street)
🍴 Cafés, tavernas (€) in Nafsikas and Dimokratias
🚌 2 Kanóni. Blue bus from San Rocco Square. Get off at Nafsikas Street
💷 Free; donations welcome
↔ Ruined Basilica of Palaiopolis (➤ 40)
❓ Sober clothing should be worn

Above: *the ancient Byzantine Church of St Jason and St Sosipater*

✚ 32A3
✉ Kolokotroni, off Mitropolitou Methodiou
🕐 All day
🍴 Cafés, restaurants (€–€€) in Mitropolitou Methodiou
♿ Accessible to wheelchairs

32C5

✉ Paláti tou Agíou Michaíl tou Georgíou (Palace of St Michael and St George, East Wing)

🕐 Tue–Sat 8:30–3, Sun 9:30–2:30

🍴 Art Gallery Café (€), behind the palace

♿ None

💰 Moderate

↔ Palace of St Michael and St George (➤ 40), Old Fortress (➤ 39)

Above: The Assassination of Capodistrias, *by Charalambos Pachis*

DIMOTIKÍ PINAKOTHÍKI (MUNICIPAL ART GALLERY) ⭐⭐

This delightful gallery was opened in 1995 in the east wing of the Palace of St Michael and St George. The exhibition rooms are a pleasure in themselves, and the approach, through a serene, tree-shaded garden and past the Art Café and Bar, is charming. The works in the gallery are mainly by 19th- and 20th-century Corfiot painters and sculptors, but there are also medieval paintings including the powerful *Decapitation of John The Baptist* by Michael Damaskinos. Notable Corfiot painters include Charalambos Pachis, whose *The Assassination of Capodistrias* is a touch melodramatic, but compelling. The French-influenced painting of the Liston, *Night in Corfu* (1913), by George Samartzis has a happy relevance for holiday-makers. Modern works by the engraver Nikolaos Ventouras, and later abstract paintings by Aglaia Papa, are also on display. Next to the café-bar there is another smaller gallery, which stages various exhibitions.

32B5

✉ 120 Kapodistriou Street

🕐 Mon–Fri 10–1:30

🍴 Art Gallery Café (€) behind the Palace of St Michael and St George

💰 Free

↔ Palace of St Michael and St George (➤ 40)

❓ Not formally open to the public, but researchers and visitors with a genuine interest are welcome

KERKURAIKÍ ANAGNOSTIKÍ ETAIRÍA (CORFU READING SOCIETY) ⭐

This venerable Society was founded in 1836 by a group of young Corfiot intellectuals, giving it a claim to being the oldest cultural institution in modern Greece. The Society's premises are in a handsome Venetian building at the south end of Arseniou near the Palace of St Michael and St George. Its arcaded façade incorporates an outside staircase and an upper verandah. At street level, a small relief of an owl, symbol of wisdom, strikes a charming and witty note.

The interior of the building has the comfortable, well-worn atmosphere of all good libraries; the walls are hung with paintings and prints. There is an impressive collection of Ionian-related books, manuscripts, periodicals, engravings, maps and other material by Greek and foreign authors. Researchers and interested visitors are welcomed with great courtesy.

Corfu's cathedral (left), is home to St Theodora's remains, suitably housed in a beautifully worked silver casket (below)

MITRÓPOLI (CATHEDRAL)

Corfu's Orthodox cathedral, the Cathedral of Panagia Spiliotissa (Madonna of the Grotto), stands at the top of a flight of steps set back from the Old Port Square. The 16th-century building, which did not become a cathedral until 1841, is dedicated to St Theodora Augusta, whose mummified remains were brought to Corfu at the same time as those of the more celebrated St Spyrídon. The saint's remains now lie in a silver casket in the cathedral.

The interior of the cathedral is rather sombre, lined with dark wooden panelling and hung with candelabra. There is a white iconostasis with a broken pediment, and the numerous icons include a beautiful image of the Archangel Michael and another of the Virgin.

32B5

Plateia Konstantinou, off Old Port Square

Daily 9–2. Avoid casual visits during services

Cafés, restaurants (€–€€) in Old Port Square

Free, donations welcome

Old Port Square (➤ 41)

Sober clothing should be worn. Ceremony on first Sunday of Lent when relics of St Theodora are carried round town

MON REPOS

The elegant villa of Mon Repos was built on a choice site on the Kanóni Peninsula in 1831 for the British High Commissioner, Sir Frederick Adam. Its style is neo-classical, with a nod to the Byzantine in its crowning rotunda. The British ceded Mon Repos to King George I of Greece on their withdrawal from Corfu in 1864. Prince Philip, Duke of Edinburgh, was born here in 1921.

The house had a chequered history in subsequent years and lay neglected as legal disputes dragged on between the former King Constantine of Greece and the Municipality of Corfu. The latter has restored the property, which is now fully open to the public.

At the south end of the wooded grounds are the impressive ruins of a Doric temple of about 500 BC.

32C1

Nafsikas, Anemomylos

Daily 9–9, off-season 9–4

Cafés, tavernas (€–€€) in nearby Garítsa

2 Kanóni. Blue bus from San Rocco Square

None

Grounds free, villa moderate

Christian Basilica of Palaiopolis (➤ 40)

MOUSEÍO ARCHAIOLOGIKÓ (ARCHAEOLOGICAL MUSEUM) (► 23, TOP TEN)

MOUSEÍO SOLOMOÚ (SOLOMOS MUSEUM) ✪

The poet Dionysios Solomos (1798–1857) was born on the island of Zakynthos but spent his later life on Corfu. He championed the modern Greek language, and in 1863 the first two stanzas of his 1822 poem, 'Hymn to Liberty', were set to music by his friend, the composer Nicholas Mantzaros. The combined work became the Greek national anthem. Goethe described Solomos as the 'Byron of the East'. The Solomos Museum, just off Arseniou, is a reconstruction of the house in which Solomos lived and which was destroyed by bombs during World War II. A visit to the museum may prove frustrating for visitors without knowledge of Greek, but the atmosphere alone is rewarding.

MOUSEÍO VIZANTINÓ ✪✪✪
(BYZANTINE MUSEUM)

The Church of Panagia Antivouniotissa (Church of the Blessed Virgin – the name Antivouniotissa comes from the hill on which the church stands), which houses this outstanding collection of Byzantine art, dates from the 16th century. There are about 90 icons on display, most from the 13th to the 17th centuries and depicting individual saints and biblical scenes. There is also outstanding work by the celebrated Cretan painters Emanuel Tzanes and Michael Damaskinos, among others. The plain outside walls of the church mask a beautiful interior of enclosed arcades surrounding a central nave with a wonderful coffered and decorated ceiling, painted walls and gilded woodwork. From the centre of the nave, the view through the glass entrance door to Vídos Island in the distance makes an exquisite picture.

One of the many superb icons in Corfu Town's Byzantine Museum

✚ 32B5
✉ 3rd Parados, Arseniou
☎ (06610) 30674
🕐 Jun–Oct 9:30–2;
Nov–May 9:30–1
🍴 Cafés, restaurants (€–€€) in Old Port Square
♿ None
💰 Moderate
↔ Byzantine Museum (► below)
❓ Labels are in Greek only

✚ 32B5
✉ Arseniou (Mourayia)
☎ (06610) 38313
🕐 Tue–Sun 8:30–3
🍴 Cafés, restaurants (€–€€) in Old Port Square, Faliraki (€€)
💰 Moderate
↔ Solomos Museum (► above)
❓ Exhibits generally labelled in English as well as Greek

A Walk into the Past

Many historic monuments are passed on this walk through the southern part of Corfu Town.

Start at the Peristýlio Maitland (Maitland Rotunda, ➤ 47). Walk south and cross the road diagonally left. Continue south on Dimokratias, alongside the sea, for 1.7km to reach the small harbour at Anemomylos. Continue until you arrive opposite the Hotel Mon Repos. Cross the road, with care, then go down the lane to the left of the hotel. Pass Ágios Iásonas kai Sosipátros (the Byzantine Church of St Jason and St Sosipater, ➤ 33) on the left.

Continue on to the junction with Nafsikas Street. Turn right and, where the road widens, turn right again and cross into the tree-shaded walkway nearest the coast. Follow this north for about 1km to reach Oveliskos Ntalklas (the Douglas Obelisk). Cross left to Proxenío Anglías (the British Consulate).

The Maitland Rotunda at the south end of the Spianáda (Esplanade)

The obelisk commemorates General Sir Howard Douglas, the 4th British High Commissioner, an able administrator.

Go up Menekrátous Street to the left of the consulate. At a junction of five roads, cross diagonally left to a brick building behind railings in Kyprou (Cyprus) Street.

Stíli tou Menekráti (the Tomb of Menekrates) is to the left of the building. This 6th-century cenotaph celebrates Menekrates, a representative of ancient Corcyra.

Continue along Kyprou (Cyprus) Street for about 100m, then go sharp right on to a road rising through trees. Continue until you reach a T-junction by the walls of Corfu Prison. Turn left and follow the walls round past the prison gate and on down Kolokotroni Street to Anglikó Nekrotafeío (the British Cemetery, ➤ 33). Continue on to a busy junction with Mitropolitou Methodiou. Turn right and continue to San Rocco Square.

Distance
5km

Time
1½ hours

Start point
Maitland Rotunda
✚ 32B4

End point
San Rocco Square
✚ 32A4

Lunch
Cafés and tavernas
✉ Mitr Athanassiou (€)

The approach to the Néo Froúrio, the imposing New Fortress of the 16th century

 32A5
✉ Solomos Street, off Spilia Square or New Fortress Square
☎ (06610) 27477
🕐 May–Oct daily 9–9
🍴 Cafés, tavernas (€–€€) in nearby Old Port Square
♿ None
💵 Moderate
↔ Old Port (➤ 41)

The Lion of St Mark, the famous arms of Venice above a gateway to the Néo Froúrio

NÉO FROÚRIO (NEW FORTRESS) ⭐

The New Fortress is 'new' only in the sense that it was started in 1572, a mere 15 years after the Venetians began rebuilding the Old Fortress. The massive outerworks of this 'Néo Froúrio' were built by the Venetians, but the buildings that survive within the walls, a mass of tunnels, vaulted chambers and stairways, were added by the British. On its eastern side are two entrances: an unused one in Solomou Square, resplendent with a relief of the Venetian winged Lion of St Mark; the other, in New Fortress Square, is the military gate, used by the resident Naval authorities. Public entrance is via the steep stone steps that lead up from the far end of the square past the Roman Catholic Church of Tenedos. There are fine views from the bastions and at the top a café/bar, exhibition centre and small museum of ceramics (although this is not always open).

> ### *Did you know ?*
>
> *There is a maze of tunnels, excavated by the Venetians, beneath the Old Fortress and the New Fortress in Corfu Town. One tunnel is said to run beneath the sea to Vídos Island, which lies just offshore from the town. Vídos was strategically important to both attack on the town and, when fortified, to its defence. There are various ruins on the island and a mausoleum commemorating Serbian soldiers who died of plague during World War I.*

NÉO LIMANI (NEW PORT) ✪

The area of the New Port is neither scenic nor tourist-orientated, but it is a lively place, full of everyday activities and the rattle and hum of seagoing vessels. Boats, large and small, throng the working harbour, while the big mainland and island ferries come and go along the quays further north. The busy seafront road is lined with ships' chandlers, marine suppliers and workshops, as well as travel agencies and car-hire firms. At the western end is the old district of Mandouki, with its cafés and tavernas.

➕ 32A5
✉ Ethnikis Antistasseos
🕐 Daily 9–2
🍴 Cafés, tavernas, fast-food shops (€–€€) in nearby Mandouki
🚢 Main port for big ferries
💰 Free
↔ Monastery of Platitéra (➤ 44), Old Port (➤ 41)

PALAIÓ FROÚRIO (OLD FORTRESS) ✪✪

The Old Fortress, is a powerful visual symbol of town and island. The earliest known fortifications were Byzantine, established in the 6th century after the destruction of the old Corinthian city of Palaiopolis (➤ 40) by Goth raiders. The Venetians replaced and extended the walls in the 15th century and excavated the defensive moat, the Contrafossa, that now adds such a picturesque element to the scene. Further rebuilding took place between 1558 and 1588, and it is these fortifications that survive today.

The fortress is approached from the east side of the Esplanade. The right-hand guardhouse in the main gatehouse houses the Byzantine Collection of Corfu with mosaics and sculptures from the Basilica of Palaiopolis. There are fresco fragments from St Nicholas's church in Kato Korakiana. Across the bridge is the Church of the Madonna of the Carmelites. The summit of the inner peak, the 'Castel a Terra' or Landward Castle, with its little light-house, can be reached by a steep climb past a Venetian clock-tower. At 72m high, the view over Corfu Town and inland to Mount Pandokrator (➤ 26) is spectacular.

➕ 32C4
✉ Spianáda (Esplanade)
☎ (06610) 48310
🕐 May–Oct daily 8–7, Nov–Apr daily 8:30–3
🍴 Art Gallery Café (€)
🚫 None
💰 Expensive
↔ Municipal Art Gallery (➤ 34), Palace of St Michael and St George (➤ 40), Esplanade (➤ 46)

The neo-classical Church of St George, at the heart of the Old Fortress, was built by the British as a garrison church

PALAIOPOLIS (ANCIENT CITY OF CORCYRA) ✪✪

Poignant relics of Palaiopolis, the ancient city of Corcyra, survive on the Kanóni Peninsula 5km south of Corfu Town. One of the oldest ruins is the Tower of Nerandzicha, a remnant of the city walls dating from the 5th century BC. Near by are the impressive remains of the late 6th-century BC Temple of Artemis, from which the Gorgon pediment, now housed in Corfu Town's Archaeological Museum (➤ 23), was recovered.

On the road to Kanóni, opposite the gates to Mon Repos (➤ 35), are the ruins of the 5th-century Christian Basilica of Palaiopolis. Near by are the substantial ruins of Roman baths of about AD 200.

- ✚ 28B4
- ✉ Anemomylos
- 🍴 Cafés, tavernas (€–€€) in nearby Garitsa
- 🚌 2 Kanóni. Blue bus from San Rocco Square
- ♿ Free
- ↔ Mon Repos (➤ 35)

PALÁTI TOU AGÍOU MICHAÍL TOU GEORGÍOU ✪✪✪
(PALACE OF ST MICHAEL AND ST GEORGE)

Dominating the Plateía, the northern end of the Esplanade, the palace is the most striking relic of the 50-year British presence on Corfu. It was built between 1819 and 1824 under Sir Thomas Maitland, the first High Commissioner, and was used as the official seat of the Protectorate. The palace is triumphantly neo-classical in style, the first building of its kind to be built in modern Greece, with a passing nod to the Parthenon in its Doric portico. In the landscaped garden in front of the palace stands a statue of Sir Frederick Adam, second High Commissioner.

The palace was the venue for the EC Summit of 1994. The interior is outstanding: the finest feature is the rotunda on the first floor, its domed ceiling painted in blue and gold, its walls punctuated with mahogany doors, niches and mirrored panels.

Several of the state rooms house the Museum of Asiatic Art, a remarkable collection of Sino-Japanese art and artefacts, including mosaics from the early Christian Basilica of Palaiopolis (➤ 40). Chinese and Japanese exhibits make up the largest part of the collection but there are also objects

- ✚ 32C5
- ✉ Spianáda (Esplanade)
- ☎ (06610) 30443
- 🕐 Tue–Sun 8.30–3
- 🍴 Art Gallery Café (€)
- 💰 Moderate
- ↔ New Fortress (➤ 38), Old Fortress (➤ 39), Esplanade (➤ 46)

from India, Tibet, Nepal, Korea and Thailand. Items include prehistoric bronzes, porcelain ware, woodcarvings, Noh theatre masks, wood and brass statuettes, Samurai armour and weapons, screens, fans and much more. The main bulk of the collection was given to the Greek government in 1926 by the Corfiot-born diplomat Gregorios Manos (1850–1929). The palace also houses the Municipal Art Gallery (► 34) and the Modern Art Museum, containing a small collection of Greek contemporary art.

Above: the Palace of St Michael and St George houses an impressive Asiatic art museum

PALÉO LIMANI (OLD PORT) ✪✪

There is an unassuming charm about the Old Port which reflects its historic role as a maritime and commercial centre. Old Port Square was once used for the town market, and local people still gather here to gossip and relax. The quays are used for car parking, but the inner square has been landscaped and is lined with some fine old buildings, including the Law Courts and the pre-war Constantinople Hotel. Lanes and alleyways lead intriguingly into the old town from here.

Behind the Law Courts and beside the Averof Restaurant is a splendid medieval relic, the gate of the Venetian Granary, complete with a stone relief of the trireme, or rowing galley – the emblem of Old Corfu. The right-hand side of Old Port Square leads into Solomou Square and then into Spilia Square, or New Fortress Square, and so to the New Fortress; the district is still called Ovriaki from its time as the Jewish Quarter.

There are a number of unfussy cafés and tavernas along the south side of Old Port Square, below where Donzelot Street, named in honour of the popular French Governor of 1807–14, leads up to the area known as the Mourayia and into Arseniou Street. Here, magnificent Venetian buildings, as well as the Solomos Museum and the Byzantine Museum, look out across to Vídos Island.

➕ 32A5
✉ Spilia
🍴 Cafés, tavernas (€–€€)
🚢 Ferry port for Paxoi and excursions
🎟 Free
🔄 Cathedral of Panagia Spiliotissa (► 35), New Fortress (► 38), Solomos Museum (► 36), Byzantine Museum (► 36)

Left: the evocative ruins of Palaiopolis
Bottom left: Sir Thomas Maitland, first British High Commissioner of Corfu

+ 32B5
🍴 Café Plakada (€€)
♿ Good access
↔ Church of St Spyrídon
 (➤ 17)

Paper Money Museum
✉ St Spyrídon's Square
☎ (06610) 41552
🕐 Mon–Sat 9–1
🍴 Café Plakada (€€)
♿ None
💰 Moderate

PLATEÍA AGÍOU SPYRÍDONA (ST SPYRÍDON'S SQUARE)

This attractive Italianate square lies at the heart of Corfu Town. Its official name is Plateía Iroon Kypriakou Agonos, the Square of the Heroes of the Cypriot Struggle, but the nearby Church of St Spyrídon has given it the more manageable name of St Spyrídon's Square, or the Saint's Square. Two other churches stand near by, the Church of the Virgin of Strangers, so-called because it is the parish church of mainland Greeks, and the Church of St John the Baptist, or St John at the Cisterns, named after the rainwater tanks that once lay beneath the square. On the western side of the square is the handsome classical façade of the 19th-century Ionian Bank, designed by the Corfiot architect John Chronis (1799–1879). To the right of the bank is the Mouseío Hartovomismáton (**Paper Money Museum**), which has a unique collection of historic Greek banknotes and an exhibition explaining their production.

PLATEÍA DEMARCHÍOU (TOWN HALL SQUARE) ★★

Known officially as Plateía Demarchíou, this attractive central square, where there are several craft shops and pâtisseries, descends in a series of paved terraces from south to north. At the centre stands a bust of Iakovos Polylas (1825–93), friend of the poet Dionysios Solomos, and himself a distinguished writer and translator. Guilford Street, named after Frederick North, fifth Earl of Guilford, leads into the square. Guilford was a genial eccentric and enthusiastic Grecophile who converted to Greek Orthodoxy and brought to fruition John Capodistrias's dream of an Ionian Academy, the first university in modern Greece.

The focus of the square is Corfu Town Hall, an intriguing building that has undergone a number of transformations since its origins in the late 17th century as an open arcade, the Loggia dei Nobili, a meeting place of the Venetian hierarchy. It was subsequently converted to a theatre, and a second floor was added when it became the Town Hall in 1903. On the east wall is a spectacular marble relief depicting Francesco Morosini – Venetian Admiral (later Doge of Venice), Hammer of the Turks in the Peloponnese, and incidental demolisher of the Athenian Parthenon when he bombarded the Turkish-held Acropolis in 1687 (the Parthenon was the Turk's gunpowder store). Morosini glares threateningly at the handsome façade of the Roman Catholic Cathedral of St James and St Christopher diagonally opposite. The original St James's was a parish church of 1588 and became a cathedral in 1633. After much damage from bombing in 1943, the present building was restored.

✚ 32B4
🍴 Arpi (€€) just off Town Hall Square
✋ Free

This dramatic relief of Francesco Morosini dominates the side of Corfu Town Hall

Left: *a relaxed sunlit scene in St Spyrídon's Square defines the spirit of Corfu Town*

43

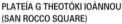

➕ 32A4
🍴 Cafés, restaurant, fast-
food outlets (€–€€)

PLATEÍA G THEOTÓKI IOÁNNOU (SAN ROCCO SQUARE) ✪

Corfu Town's commercial heart is as brash and traffic-bound as central Athens. But it does have a heart. The central plaza has seating, though a pause for quiet reflection is not an option, and busy shopping streets radiate from all corners. There are numerous hot-food shops and several *periptero* kiosks along the north side. The Blue Bus terminus is on the southeast side. Polihroni Konstanda Street leads off the west corner of San Rocco and, though heavy with traffic, is worth exploring for its arcaded walkways and food shops. Mitropolitou Methodiou Street leads southwest, and the attractive Alexandras Avenue, with a number of pavement cafés, leads southeast. G Theotoki Street leads northeast into the old town past some wonderful shops, especially on its south side. Do not miss the morning market, reached up Gerasimou Markora Street on the north side of San Rocco Square.

PLATITÉRA (MONASTERY OF THE VIRGIN) ✪

Platitéra, meaning 'Wider than the Heavens', is an oasis of calm alongside Corfu Town's busy link road to the coast road north: traffic hurtles past the palm-filled little entrance courtyard and its tall, red-domed bell-tower. Although the original 18th-century convent was set on fire by the French in 1798 in response to a revolt against them by local people, it was soon rebuilt. There are very fine icons and paintings inside the church, although the poor light does not do them justice. The most dramatic are *The Day of Judgement*, by the 16th-century Cretan painter George Klotzas, and the *Allegory of Heavenly Jerusalem*, or, more pointedly, *The Damned and the Blessed*, by an unknown 16th-century artist. The latter brims with graphic symbols of wickedness. Behind the sanctuary is the tomb of Count John Capodistrias.

➕ 32A4
✉ Andreadi
🕐 Daily 9–2
🍴 Cafés, tavernas (€–€€) in nearby Mandouki
♿ Free, but donations welcomed
🚌 New Port (► 39)
❓ Sober clothing should be worn

Above: *lively scene in Corfu Town's old market*
Right: *the peaceful courtyard of the Monastery of Platitéra*

44

A Walk through the Campiello

A short stroll through the oldest part of Corfu Town, visiting St Spyrídon's Church and the Byzantine Museum. Start at St Spyrídon's Square, off Theotoki Nikiforou, where the Paper Money Museum (➤ 42) can be visited.

Leave the square by its far left-hand corner to reach the Church of St Spyrídon (➤ 17). Go left at the church door and down Kalogeretou beneath a vaulted archway. At the junction, go right along Filarmonikis.

Filarmonikis, unsurprisingly, is where Corfu Town's Philharmonic Societies have their rehearsal rooms.

Continue ahead up steps into Sophocleous Dousmani. Keep right and go up into Plateía Ag Elenis, with its big central palm tree. Leave the square by its far left-hand corner, turn left immediately , then right. Pass a supermarket, then turn left down steps to Plateía Taxiarchón.

On the right is the 16th-century Church of Christ Pandocrator. It has a fine doorway and a sculpted angel on the gable.

Go through the square and, beyond the little central shrine, go left and down three steps to pass through a narrow alleyway. Turn right up the next alleyway and climb steps into Plateía Kremasti (Kremasti Square) to the Venetian Well and the Church of the Virgin Kremasti.

The well-head at the centre of the square is a survivor from the medieval period.

Leave the square by the far corner of the church, then turn left and then right into a square with a huge central palm tree. Keep right of the tree, then turn right along a lane past a bell-tower. At the T-junction, go left, then, after a few metres, go left again and continue to the Byzantine Museum (➤ 36). Go right down steps to Arseniou. Turn right, follow the seafront road to where a gate gives access to the arched gate of St George, and continue to the Esplanade.

Distance
2km

Time
2 hours, if Paper Money Museum, churches, and Byzantine Museum are visited

Start point
St Spyrídon's Square
✚ 32B5

End point
Spianáda (Esplanade)
✚ 32B5

Lunch
Crêperie Christa's (€)
✉ Sophocleous Dousmani
☎ (06610) 40227

The Venetian Well and the Church of the Virgin Kremasti, old Corfu Town

THE SPIANÁDA (ESPLANADE) AND THE LISTON

Corfu Town's Esplanade is one of the most charming urban open spaces in the Mediterranean, a public arena for relaxed promenading, for reading newspapers, for quiet gossip over Greek or iced coffee, orange juice or ouzo, for carnival and festival, and for the joy of uninterrupted summer sunshine from morning till night.

The Esplanade owes its open nature to the Venetians, who cleared the medieval town that lay in front of the fortress. They ensured that the line of their buildings along the western edge of this open ground incorporated numerous straight alleyways to allow direct lines of fire from the Old Fortress to defend against potential attack from the landward side.

These buildings survive along Kapodistriou Street, but on the Plateía, the northern section of the Esplanade, the terrace of arcaded buildings known as the Liston was built by the French in the style of the Parisian rue de Rivoli. Today, with its generally expensive, but stylish, cafés and restaurants, the Liston is a focus for Corfu Town at play, a venue for a colourful mix of gregarious locals, visitors and fashion-conscious youngsters on parade. At the far end of the Esplanade is the wide green space used for cricket matches. The game is a legacy of the British who also left a taste for *tsin tsin birra* – ginger beer.

The southern half of the Esplanade is landscaped with flowerbeds and a fountain, and an elegant bandstand where the town's brass bands perform on summer Sunday

Above: *underneath the arches of the Liston*
Right: *the quieter northern end of the Esplanade*

The classic French style of the Liston, the place for promenading

afternoons. At its far end is the Peristýlio Maitland (Maitland Rotunda), a rather battered classical memorial built in honour of Sir Thomas Maitland, the first High Commissioner during the British Protectorate.

Did you know?

The British unwittingly stimulated Corfu's marvellous tradition of Philharmonic Societies when, in 1837, the British High Commissioner prohibited military bands from taking part in religious ceremonies. Until then a British military band had accompanied the annual St Spyrídon procession. In response to a silent procession, local musicians founded the St Spyrídon Philharmonic Society and by 1841 were performing in full uniform.

Around the Island

Beyond the olive groves, Corfu is an island of hidden contrasts. The northwest is an area of discovery, where roads lead enticingly to invigorating beaches, or to the edge of towering cliffs. The northeast is centred on the mighty Mount Pandokrator, whose wilder reaches offer an escape from the crowds and whose rocky eastern slopes drop steeply to quiet coves and dazzling shingle beaches. Central Corfu boasts the beautiful west coast resorts and the remoteness of tree-covered mountains, while the low-lying south has miles of peaceful west-facing beaches and more of those fascinating villages where the life of Old Corfu goes on unhindered. To experience the essence of Corfu you need to do some planning. A hire car gives independence, but responsibility. A stress-free alternative for getting about is the island's rural bus service. And walking can be combined with bus connections to get even closer to traditional Corfu.

'Yet the more I see of this place, so the more I feel that no other spot on earth can be fuller of beauty, and variety of beauty.'

EDWARD LEAR
describing Corfu in a letter,
March 1862

———————●———————

What to See Around the Island

ACHARÁVI ★

A popular family resort on Corfu's north coast, Acharávi lies a short distance inland from the beach and to either side of the wide and dusty main road. The wooded heights of Mount Pandokrator rise impressively behind and a different world of dense olive groves and quiet villages, such as Epískepsi and Láfki, can be quickly, if steeply, reached from the resort.

Acharávi has a range of shops and eating places. Villas and hotels fill the space between village and seafront. The sand and shingle beach shelves gently and bathing is safe. Watersports are available here, and there are beachside cafés and tavernas. The remote Paralía Almyroú (Almirós Beach) lies at the east end of Acharávi's long strand. This is less crowded but the shoreline has low mudstone reefs, which children may find awkward and slippy.

AFIÓNAS ★

The road ends at Afiónas. Go any further and you would fall into the sea. To the south of the village lies a narrow promontory that ends at Ákrotírio (Cape) Aríllas, while to the west lies Kravía (Gravia) Island, the 'Ship Island', with its little flotilla of offshore rocks trailing behind it. From opposite the church at Afiónas a path leads down the spine of the promontory. Halfway along at a narrow neck of scrubby land that links the rocky hills of the ridge is the small cove of Porto Timoni. Small beaches lie to either side and you can switch from one to the other depending on wind direction. On the headland are the faint remains of defensive walls, which date from about 500 BC. Excavations in 1912 uncovered traces of a neolithic settlement dating from 3000 BC.

✚	28B5
✉	38km north of Corfu Town, on north coast main road
🍴	Beachside tavernas and cafés (€–€€)
🚌	Green bus from Avramiou Street, Corfu Town–Acharávi
🚢	Day trips to the Diapondia island of Erikoussa
♿	Beach accessible from seafront road
↔	Ágios Spyrídon (► 54), Róda (► 86)
❓	Limited parking on beachfront

✚	28A5
✉	On headland on northwest coast
🍴	The Blue House (€€) just before entrance to village
🚌	Green bus from Avramiou Street, Corfu Town–Magouládes–Afiónas. Not Sun
↔	Ágios Geórgios (northwest) (► 50)
❓	Limited parking

The exhilarating colours of Corfu at the village of Afiónas

49

28A5
✉ On shores of bay on northwest coast
🍴 Tavernas and restaurants (€–€€) throughout the resort
🚌 Green bus from Avramiou Street, Corfu Town–Ágios Geórgios
↔ Afiónas (➤ 49)
❓ Limited parking on beachside road

🞤 28B2
✉ On the southwest coast
🍴 Several good restaurants and tavernas (€–€€) or Kafesas (€€€) for seafood at the south end of the resort
🚌 Green bus from Avramiou Street, Corfu Town–Argirádes–Ágios Geórgios
↔ Lake Korissión (➤ 22)
❓ Limited roadside parking

The exquisite beach at Ágios Górdis is framed by tree-clad mountains

ÁGIOS GEÓRGIOS (NORTHWEST)

Ágios Geórgios is an attractive northwest coast resort and although its individuality has been blurred by beachfront development, bold, natural surroundings still dominate the scene. The sandy beach sweeps for over 2km along the curve of a south-facing bay between Ákrotírio (Cape) Aríllas and Ákrotírio (Cape) Falakron.

Bathing is safe here, although the area can be windy at times, making Ágios Geórgios a good windsurfing centre. There are windsurfing schools on the beach as well as jet-ski and waterski facilities.

Just inland lies Págoi (Pagi), a traditional Corfiot village, whose narrow lanes were not made for the motor car.

ÁGIOS GEÓRGIOS (SOUTHWEST)

Like its northern namesake, this Ágios Geórgios has been tacked on to a long stretch of sandy beach, part of the almost continuous 12km strand that fringes the southwest shoreline of Corfu. Linear development has left the resort without much heart, but location is what matters. Numerous watersports are available at Ágios Geórgios and there are several good tavernas overlooking the beach. The beach is narrow, but you can find uncrowded space if you are willing to walk some distance along the open coast in either direction.

On the main road, inland, is the large village of Argyrádes (Argirádes), worth visiting for its friendly, down-to-earth atmosphere, its Venetian architecture and its shops and cafés.

ÁGIOS-GÓRDIS ✪✪

This is an attractive west coast resort at the foot of spectacular pine-covered coastal hills. The beach is framed by big headlands to north and south. At the northern end of the beach are Plitiri Point and the rocky heights of Aerostato, known at one time as 'The Lookout' because of its use as a watch-point for pirates and potential invaders. Just offshore from Ágios Górdis's southern headland is a remarkable tusk-like pinnacle called the Ortholith. Onshore is a similar pinnacle, beyond which rises the great bulk of Mount Garoúna. The beach is wide and sandy with patches of shingle, and numerous watersports are available, including a beachside diving centre. A steep hike to the south from Ágios Górdis takes you to the rocky cove of Fieroula and on to the hamlet of Pentátion.

ÁGIOS MATTAÍOS (ÁGIOS MATTHÉOS) ✪

There is an enduring belief that in Ágios Matthéos local people are descended from the Byzantine defenders of nearby Gardíki Castle (➤ 68). The village, one of the largest and most traditional of Corfu's mountain villages, is built on a series of terraces on the tree-covered slopes of the 463m Mount Ágios Matthéos, known locally as Grava. Near the top of the mountain is the 4th-century Monastery of Pandokrator, now abandoned but cared for by villagers. On 6 August each year a religious festival is held here through the night. A paved lane winds through the heart of the village to a wide square with a fountain and a beautifully kept church. The view east across the island from here is exhilarating.

✚ 28B3
✉ 17km southwest of Corfu Town
🍴 Cafés and tavernas (€–€€) throughout the resort
🚌 Green bus from Avramiou Street, Corfu Town–Ágios Górdis
↔ Sinarádes (➤ 90)
❓ Limited parking

Above: *traditional Corfu survives in the delightful village of Ágios Matthéos*

✚ 28B3
✉ 22km southwest of Corfu Town
🍴 Snack bars (€) in main street
🚌 Green bus from Avramiou Street, Corfu Town–Ágios Matthéos
↔ Gardíki Castle (➤ 68)
❓ A small car park on the northern edge of the village, signposted

In the Know

If you only have a short time to spend on Corfu, or would like to get a real flavour of the island, here are some ideas:

10
Ways to Be a Local

Take time over your taverna meals. Talk a great deal, without inhibitions. Be demonstrative.

Buy worry beads, known as *kombologi*. (Unfortunately bead-worrying is an entirely male habit, which is a worry in itself.)

Drink *Ellinikos kafes,* Greek coffee. Take small sips and top up with water. Alternatively, brace yourself for ouzo; potent, but very Greek. Never add water to the glass. Instead match ouzo and water, sip for sip.

Prise yourself off the sun lounger (if the ouzo hasn't won). Head into the hills on foot, or visit one of Corfu's enchanting inland villages, such as Doukádes, Lefkimmi or Ágios Matthéos.

Go fishing off the Old Port quays. Use a small hook, a light line and bread paste for bait. If you catch anything, act as if nothing has happened, but casually wave the fish in the air for a second or two.

Enjoy *kafes frappe* (iced coffee) in the Liston of a morning. Haggle over the price – if you dare.

Wear sober clothing and visit at least one of Corfu's many historic country churches.

Look out for a local carnival or festival and merge with the crowd. Suspend any plans for the rest of the day; and the night for that matter.

Keep your head high, eyes constantly swivelling right to left, and move very fast when negotiating pedestrian crossings in the San Rocco Square area of Corfu Town.

Accept, of course, that you are not a local, but get close to the experience by appreciating the spirited and generous lifestyle of the Corfiots.

10
Good Places to Have Lunch

La Famiglia (€–€€)
✉ 30 Maniarizi Arlioti Street ☎ (06610) 30270. Italian café-restaurant. Imaginative snacks and light meals on a busy, colourful street.

Gallini (€€)
✉ Ágios Stéfanos ☎ (06630) 81492. Highly popular waterfront taverna. Good steaks, *kheftiko* and other Greek dishes.

Gondola (€€)
✉ The Liston, Corfu Town ☎ (06610) 36829. Good pizzas and snacks in this most stylish setting in Corfu Town.

Great Shakes (€)
✉ Dassiá, on main road. The English proprietors serve lunch, or late breakfast. Beer from the barrel, if you're missing it.

Janis (€–€€) ✉ Kassiópi ☎ (06630) 81082. Good menu with big selection. Friendly, seafront location.

Sea Breeze (€€) ✉ Ágios Górdis ☎ (06610) 53214. Popular taverna overlooking the sea. Good Corfiot cuisine and party nights

Symposium (€€–€€€)
✉ Ágios Stéfanos. Well researched menu of ancient Greek cooking, beautifully presented. Also classic and unusual Corfiot and Greek dishes, plus Ina's own creations.

Taverna Kouloúra (€)
✉ Kouloúra ☎ (06630) 91253. Good food in an idyllic setting.

Venetian Well (€€€)
✉ Plateia Kremasti (Kremasti Square) ☎ (06610) 44761. Innovative cuisine served in an elegant restaurant.

Zack's (€) ✉ Ágios Geórgios (southwest) ☎ (06620) 52418. Good home-cooking in a garden setting.

Left: *refreshments in the morning sun*

Traditional dancers in Corfu Town

10
Best Viewpoints

- Kaiser's Lookout above Pélekas (➤ 82)
- Mount Pandokrator (➤ 26)
- Ákrotírio Drástis (➤ 86)
- Angelókastro Fortress (➤ 18)
- Bella Vista above Paleokastritsa (➤ 24)
- Mount Ágios Matthéos (➤ 51)
- Either side of the Troumbetas Pass (➤ 87)

- From the top of the Old Citadel in Corfu Town
- On the road from Spartýlas to the coast (➤ 57)
- Mount Ágios Déka (➤ 12)

10
Mementoes of Corfu

- Lace from Kassiópi
- Bottle of kumquat liqueur (➤ panel 107) and crystallised kumquats
- A subtle suntan
- A small bottle of ouzo with which to impress (or destroy) the taste buds of your friends back home
- Olive-wood carving
- Worry beads (*kombologi*)
- Bottle of virgin olive oil; the finest
- Leather bag, or shepherd's woven satchel
- *Baklava* (syrup cakes); *kataifi* (honey cakes); *mandolato* (nougat)
- Gold or silver jewellery

Kassiópi lace-maker

10
Best Beaches

- Ágios Geórgios, northwest and southwest, for families (➤ 50)
- Ágios Stéfanos (northwest) for families and watersports (➤ 55)
- Barmpáti (Barbati): ideal for families and relatively quiet (➤ 61)
- Diapondía Islands, if you have the time to get there, for a reasonable sense of isolation (➤ 66)
- Glyfáda, for golden sand and watersports (➤ 69)
- Halikounas Beach, Lake Korissíon, for open space and peace and quiet (➤ 22)
- Kávos, for recovering from non-stop partying (➤ 73)
- Myrtiótissa, for Nature in the Raw (➤ 79)
- Sidári, for all the family, from the young to the young at heart (➤ 88)
- Ýpsos (Ipsos); crowded, but handy for bars, clubs and tavernas (➤ 90)

53

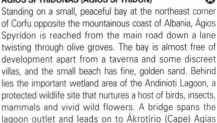

🚩 28C6

✉ On north coast 43km from Corfu Town

🍴 Tavernas at Ágios Spyrídon and at Almirós (€–€€)

❓ Limited roadside parking

Below: *fishing boats line the shore at Ágios Stéfanos on Corfu's northeast coast*

🚩 28C5

✉ 35km north of Corfu Town on northeast coast. A 3km lane leads to the village from Siniés on the main coast road

🍴 Several tavernas (€€)

🚌 Green bus from Avramiou Street, Corfu Town

🚢 Ágios Spyrídon and Kerasiá can both be reached from Kassiópi and other resorts by boat

↔ Kassiópi (▶ 72)

❓ Limited parking

ÁGIOS SPYRÍDONAS (ÁGIOS SPYRÍDON) ✪

Standing on a small, peaceful bay at the northeast corner of Corfu opposite the mountainous coast of Albania, Ágios Spyrídon is reached from the main road down a lane twisting through olive groves. The bay is almost free of development apart from a taverna and some discreet villas, and the small beach has fine, golden sand. Behind lies the important wetland area of the Andinioti Lagoon, a protected wildlife site that nurtures a host of birds, insects, mammals and vivid wild flowers. A bridge spans the lagoon outlet and leads on to Ákrotírio (Cape) Agías Aikaterínis, which is worth exploring.

Just inland from the cape, amid pine trees, is the old monastery of Agia Ekaterini (St Katherine). A track leads, in about 3km, to Paralía Almyroú (Almirós Beach).

ÁGIOS STÉFANOS (NORTHEAST) ✪✪

The fishing village of Ágios Stéfanos has kept its traditional character while adapting gracefully to its other role as a resort. Set within the arms of a quiet bay beneath tree-covered slopes, it is reached down a road which winds through olive groves, then descends through steep bends to the coast. White-walled buildings lie behind the beach, wooden jetties project into the bay, and fishing boats come and go. Early and late in the day, it feels as if the way of life that has flourished here for generations has hardly changed at all. To the east, across the narrow waters of the Corfu Channel, lies Albania, here at its closest point to Corfu. The beaches become crowded in summer when excursion boats bring day visitors from nearby Kassiópi and Kalámi. There are excursions in turn from Ágios Stéfanos, and boats can be hired for exploring

the coast and coves to either side. Beach equipment can be hired too, and some watersports are available.

Tracks and paths lead north to the isolated beach at Avláki (► 61). The road south continues through well-tended, wooded countryside criss-crossed with immaculate limestone walls. After about 1.5km it ends at the very long beach of Kerasiá. Although this is an undeveloped area – apart from a single taverna and some villas – Paralía Kerasiás (Kerasiá Beach) is very popular with day visitors who arrive in large numbers by excursion boat. By evening the beach regains a sense of pleasant isolation, though it forfeits the sun.

An 18th-century chapel at the northwest resort of Ágios Stéfanos

ÁGIOS STÉFANOS (NORTHWEST)

Corfu's other Ágios Stéfanos is a popular family resort on the northwest coast of the island, set on the shores of a wide bay with a large, flat expanse of beach and high white cliffs at the northern end of the bay. The resort, custom-built with villas, hotels, tavernas, bars and shops lining the beachfront, is named after the Chapel of San Stefano, which stands on a small promontory to the south of the beach. Beyond the chapel lies a large working harbour full of fishing caiques and excursion boats. There is safe bathing at the beach, which is crossed at its mid-point by a rather marshy river, and all types of beach equipment are on offer. Watersports include waterskiing and paragliding, and trips can be arranged to the nearby Diapondía Islands (► 66) and south to Paleokastritsa (► 24).

✚ 28A6

✉ 45km from Corfu Town on northwest coast

🍴 Gallini (€€) and Waves Taverna (€–€€)

🚌 Green bus from Avramiou Street, Corfu Town–Sidári–Ágios Stéfanos

🛳 Trips to Diapondía Islands and to Paleokastritsa

♿ Flat access to beach

↔ Arillas (► 59)

❓ Some parking on beach

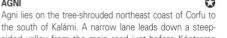

+ 28C5
⊠ 28km north of Corfu
Town on northeast coast
🍴 Taverna Agni (€€)
🚌 Green bus from Avramiou
Street, Corfu
Town–Kassiópi
🛥 Caiques from Kalámi and
from resorts to the south
↔ Kalámi (➤ 20)
❓ Parking is very difficult

AGNI ✪

Agni lies on the tree-shrouded northeast coast of Corfu to the south of Kalámi. A narrow lane leads down a steep-sided valley from the main road just before Kéntroma village but driving is not advised and it is wiser to walk down, past tiny fields and allotments, to the small shingle beach. Agni is more often reached by boat from neighbouring resorts. The tavernas here are noted for their good food and relaxed ambience, though they are popular and often busy. It is possible to walk along the coast from Agni, north to Kalámi, or south to Nissaki passing the old chapel of St Arsenious on the way.

+ 28C1
⊠ 50km south of Corfu
Town, 2km from
southern end of Kávos
🍴 Wide choice of snack-
bars, cafés in Kávos (€)
🚌 Green bus from Avramiou
Street, Corfu
Town–Kávos
♿ Not accessible
↔ Kávos (➤ 73)

Above: *olive groves
dominate the
southernmost tip of Corfu
at Cape Asprókavos*

ÁKROTÍRIO ASPRÓKAVOS (CAPE ASPRÓKAVOS) ✪

Beyond the liveliness of Kávos, with its numerous bars and clubs (➤ 73), there is an altogether different world. At the south end of the resort a road branches left to Pantatika, the final beachside extension of Kávos. Beyond, a rough track branches right into olive groves and within seconds you are in a world of shaded trees and peace and quiet – provided it is not the height of the shooting season. Keep to the main track as it winds on through deep woods of olive, cypress, ilex and oak, towards Cape Asprókavos. It reaches the coast above pale sandstone cliffs and finally leads to the ruin of the ancient Moní Panagiás (Monastery of Panagia Arkoudilla). Here, the Venetian bell-tower survives, framed between tall cypresses. Inside the building there are faded wall-paintings and a handful of icons.

A Drive Around Northeast Corfu

This is a route of dramatic contrasts, following Corfu's scenic northeast coast and returning through the mountains.

Start at the Old Port in Corfu Town. Drive west from Old Port along Xenofondos Stratigou and Eth Antistasseos. Continue along the coast road for 3km to a big junction. Go right, and after 10km, at Tzavros, turn off right, signposted Dassiá. Pass through Dassiá (➤ 65), Ipsos (➤ 90) and Barmbáti (➤ 61). Pass through Nissaki (➤ 79) and 5km further on reach the turn off for Kalámi (➤ 20).

Parking is limited at Kalámi, but there is a large lay-by on the main road just before the turn off. From here it is just under 1km to Kalámi and its neighbour, Kouloúra (➤ 74).

Continue along main road to Kassiópi (➤ 72) and on to Acharávi (➤ 49). Halfway through Acharávi's wide main street, pass a walled roundabout with an old waterpump at its centre. About 150m further on, look out for a signpost pointing left to Epískepsi and Ágios Panteleímonas. Turn left on to a narrow road. Continue steeply and through many bends (road improved in 1998 but watch for pot-holes). In 5km, reach Epískepsi.

Epískepsi is a traditional mountain village at the heart of olive-growing country.

Continue for 9km to reach Sgourádes. (Watch out for children on narrow bends through the village.) After 10km reach a junction with a road going off left, signposted Petáleia and Strinýlas (Strinilas). This road leads in about 7km to Mount Pandokrator. Divert if desired. On the main route, continue downhill to Spartýlas. In the 4km descent to the coast road there are 25 hair-raising hairpins with stunning views all the way down: concentrate. At the coast road, turn right and return to Corfu Town through Ipsos.

Distance
80km (100km if Mount Pandokrator is included)

Time
6 hours, with stops; 7–8 hours if Mount Pandokrator is included

Start/end point
Corfu Town
✚ 28C4

Lunch
Pepes (€€)
✉ Kalámi
☎ (06630) 91180

Hidden Corfu, high in the foothills of Mount Pandokrator

ÁKROTÍRIO KOMMÉNO (CAPE KOMMÉNO)

The wooded promontory of Cape Komméno encloses a small south-facing bay at the northern end of the larger Gouviá Bay. The resort's hotels and villas are at the top end of the price range, and there is a whiff of exclusiveness in the air.

Komméno has its own version of Kanóni's little church at Vlachérna (▶ 21) in the form of the church at Ypapanti on its causeway island. Several manufactured beaches lie along the wooded shores, but they are small and monopolised by hotel guests.

In 1537 and 1716, Turkish armies landed in the Cape Komméno and Gouviá area in ultimately unsuccessful bids to capture Venetian Corfu.

ALYKÉS

The Alykés salt pans, reached by road from Áno (Higher) Lefkími, lie on the eastern shore of the Bay of Lefkími. A 'trophy' monument was erected on Cape Lefkímmis, to the east, in 435 BC to celebrate a great sea victory over Corinth by the war fleet of ancient Corcyra.

The salt pans were exploited by the Venetians for years and now large numbers of migrating birds are attracted to the disused pools in spring and autumn. There is very little tourism development in the area, but a stretch of beach at Petrakis can be reached down a short lane from the minor road between Alykés and Ákrotírio (Cape) Lefkímmis. A beachfront taverna here sets out its tables on the sand.

🞤 28B4

✉ 11km north of Corfu Town. Reached from coast road north of Gouviá just after branching right from the road to Paleokastritsa

🍴 There are a number of good-quality restaurants (€€–€€€)

↔ Dassiá (▶ 65), Gouviá (▶ 69)

❓ Limited parking

🞤 28C2

✉ 32km south of Corfu Town via Áno Lefkímmi

🍴 Beachfront taverna (€) at Petrakis

♿ Petrakis Beach accessible from road end

↔ Lefkímmi (▶ 75)

❓ Parking at road end by salt pans

Above: a *popular beach on Cape Komméno*

ANGELÓKASTRO (➤ 18, TOP TEN)

ÁNO KORAKIÁNA

Áno, or upper, Korakiána is a handsome hill village with a strong Venetian element to its buildings and its churches; it even has its own Philharmonic Society. The village lies along the tree-covered foothills of the western massif of Mount Pandokrator (➤ 26). The Church of St Athanasios has an 18th-century fresco of St Spyrídon and St Athanasios banishing a dragon, the symbol of a 4th-century plague. At the village's midpoint is the entertaining façade of a house displaying the less spiritual but highly diverting sculptures of local 'popular' artist Arestides Zach Metallinos.

The road north from here zigzags madly up the curtain wall of the mountain to Sokráki and on to the aptly named Zygós (Zigós), perched on the mountain slopes and taking its name from *zigaria*, meaning 'balance'.

- 🔲 28B5
- ✉ 18km northwest of Corfu Town
- 🍴 Cafés in village (€)
- 🚌 Green bus from Avramiou Street, Corfu Town–Korakiána
- ↔ Ipsos/Pyrgi (➤ 90)
- ❓ Small car park

Below: *the glorious interior of the Church of St Athanasios at Áno Korakiána*

ARÍLLAS

This pleasant resort lies at the northern end of a long bay on the northwest coast, a few kilometres north of Ákrotírio (Cape) Aríllas. Although remote, there are plenty of resort attractions and gift shops crammed into the narrow approach road.

The narrow beach is mainly sand with patches of shingle and it has a gentle slope into the sea. The bay here can be quite breezy at times, making the resort particularly popular with windsurfers. Boards, pedaloes and canoes can be hired.

Kravía (Gravia) Island lies to the south. Like every other rocky islet off Corfu's coast, it is claimed to be the Phaeacian ship turned to stone by Poseidon in revenge for the Phaeacians transporting Odysseus home to Ithaca.

- 🔲 28A5
- ✉ 43km from Corfu Town on northwest coast. Reached from Troumbetas
- 🍴 Several tavernas and cafés (€–€€)
- 🚌 Green bus from Avramiou Street, Corfu Town–Afiónas, continues to Aríllas
- 🚢 Excursion boats to and from other resorts
- ↔ Ágios Stéfanos (northwest) (➤ 55)
- ❓ Some seafront parking

A Walk to a Spectacular View

Distance
4km

Time
2 hours

Start/end point
Doukádes
⊞ 28A5
If using your own transport, approach from the Paleokastritsa road. Go through the village to its northern end to a little car park down a slip road on the left. Walk back uphill to the village square

🚌 Green bus from Avramiou Street, Corfu Town–Paleokastritsa

Lunch
Choice of tavernas in Doukádes (€)

View from the mountain track above Doukádes

The route leads from a Corfiot mountain village through olive groves to a tiny chapel.

Start at the square in Doukádes (➤ 66). The village probably originated during a period of devastating pirate raids on Corfu's coastal communities when people retreated to the more remote interior.

Continue along the main street for 40m, then go up right between stone steps and a telegraph pole. Climb to the old church with its red-roofed apse. Keep alongside the church and go up the surfaced path.

Note the Venetian mansion on the right, complete with Italian nameplate on the wall.

When the path meets a road surfaced with ribbed concrete, go right. Follow the road as it twists and turns uphill through olive groves. Leave the road where it bends sharply right and follow the rough track ahead and continue uphill. Soon the track turns west and levels off.

This is typical olive-growing country, remote and with a variety of wild flowers in spring.

At a junction with another track turn left. Go down through olive trees, then climb uphill. After a stony section the track ends at a clearing. At the far side of this go down a narrow, rocky path to reach the tiny Chapel of St Simeon.

The chapel stands at the very edge of sheer cliffs. Take great care, of children especially, when close to the unprotected edge. There are spectacular views down to the Paleokastritsa road, south to the villages of Gardeládes and Liapádes, and to Paleokastritsa itself.

Retrace your steps along the same route back to Doukádes.

AVLÁKI

Avláki comes as something of a surprise because of its refreshing lack of development, although it can become quite busy when day visitors arrive by excursion boat. A narrow road leads from the main road past the holiday complex of Village Michael Angelo, then winds down to the coast through olive groves and open country for just over 1km. A long swathe of shingle and sand skirts the shores of a deep bay and dense olive groves cover the slopes behind. There are some villas among the trees, plus a couple of tavernas. A windsurfing club is based here and boards can be hired and tuition arranged. Kassiópi and Ágios Stéfanos are reached by paths and tracks along the coast to north and south (➤ 83).

28C5
⊠ 35km north of Corfu Town. Turn off the main coast road just before Kassiópi

🍴 Cavo Barbaro Taverna; Avláki Taverna (€–€€)

🚤 Day excursions from Kassiópi

↔ Kassiópi (➤ 72)

❓ Parking behind beach and at south end

BARMPÁTI (BARBATI)

At Barbati the steep slopes of Mount Pandokrator crowd the shoreline and leave little room for development. Behind the beach and the main road the rocky flanks of the mountain rise from dense olive groves, creating an impressive backdrop. Barbati has a long, silvery-white, shingle beach – a striking contrast to the azure sea. The beach is ideal for youngsters because it offers safe and sheltered bathing, and lies far enough below the road to escape traffic noise. There are watersports in plenty; these include waterskiing, windsurfing and parascending, with pedaloes and dinghies for the less adventurous. The village has supermarkets, gift shops and tavernas. Nightlife is limited to quiet drinks and meals; the only thing missing on this eastern shore is a view of the sunset. But there's always the sunrise…

28B5
⊠ 20km north of Corfu Town. Beach is reached down slip road at south entrance to resort

🍴 Lord Byron (€€)

🚌 Green bus from Avramiou Street, Corfu Town–Kassiópi

↔ Ipsos/Pyrgi (➤ 90)

❓ Limited parking on main road

Above: *the attractive beach at Barbati beneath the slopes of Mount Pandokrator*

61

Food & Drink

Greek cooking has languished unfairly in the shadow of French and Italian cuisine. But the best Greek tavernas know the value of traditional cooking and today, eating out, especially on this cosmopolitan island, can be a rewarding experience.

Mezedes

Mezedes, or *'mezes'* (starters) can be a feast in themselves and true *aficionados* may never get beyond them in a good taverna. They can also meet the preferences of vegetarians and vegans. *Mezes* are a communal experience to the Greeks. Everyone digs in. Try *keftedes* (spicy meat balls); *bourekakia* (meat pies); *potopoulo* (chicken portions); *saligkaria* (snails); *manitaria* (mushrooms); *spanokeftedes* (spinach balls); *dolmadakia* (vine leaves stuffed with rice); *saganáki* (fried cheese); *horta* or *tsigarelli* (wild greens tossed in oil and lemon juice); and, of course, *elies* (olives). Throw in a selection of dips such as *tzatziki* (a mix of yoghurt, garlic and cucumber), or *melitzanasalata* (aubergine and garlic), and drink wine in copious amounts…

Above: *Greek salad*
Below: *beer with a light meal*

Meat Dishes

There is a tradition of casserole cooking on Corfu. Try *pastitsada*, a Corfu speciality with an Italian touch that derives from Venetian *spezzatino*. It is created from layered pasta, meat or veal and tomato filling, with bechamel sauce, paprika, cinnamon, and cheese topping. True Corfiot *pastitsada* is made with cockerel. *Sofrito* is another Corfiot speciality. It should contain veal preferably, or beef, cooked in white sauce with olive oil, wine vinegar, garlic and onion, plus white pepper to encourage a thirst. For a good *souvlaki* (shish kebab) ask for lamb (*arnisio*), the very best. Pork (*hirinos*) *souvlaki* is also good. The best *souvlaki* is flavoured subtly with herbs. Roast lamb (*arnaki psito*), and roast kid (*katsiki sto fourno*) are not always available, but can be had in rural tavernas during festivals. And for the adventurous, how about *kokoretsi* – lamb liver, heart, kidney and tripe kebab…

Fish

Fish, as always, is expensive, but there is nothing better than fresh fish in a good *psarotaverna* (fish restaurant) or beachside venue. Try *marides* for starters; this is whitebait, fried whole in olive oil, sprinkled with lemon and accompanied by light greens. Then there is a Greek favourite, *kalamari*, fried squid; or the Italian-influenced *bianco*, a casserole of whiting, Scorpion fish, or grey mullet cooked in garlic, pepper and lemon juice. Try *bourdetto*, a selection of small fish, oven-cooked in a sauce of oil, garlic, tomato, spring onion and red pepper. A cheaper option is *xsifhia*, a kind of 'fish-kebab', with pieces of grilled swordfish sharing a skewer with tomato and onion.

Grilling squid

Drink

Ouzo is the great Greek drink for socialising, and the essential appetizer to a feast. At nearly 50 per cent alcohol, and with a strong aniseed flavour, it can shrivel the palate of the uninitiated at 50 paces. Take sparingly, with water.

Greek wines are often dismissed, but they have kept the Greeks smiling and singing for a long time. As long as you are not an ostentatious cork-sniffer, you'll find some good wines on Corfu. These include Santa Domenica, light white and red, made from *kakotrygis* grapes. Some tavernas make their own wine, *varelisio*, from the barrel and this can be extremely good. Small rural vintners produce distinctive wines such as Liapaditiko, a white wine produced in the Liapades area, near Paleokastritsa. Corfu's most famous wine is the expensive and elusive Theotoki Roppa. Retsina is a good stand-by. This is resinated wine, common throughout Greece; an acquired taste, but

A Greek banquet!

when it is good and from the barrel, it is persuasive; when it is bad, usually from the bottle, it can be wicked. Light beers and lagers are a standard drink throughout Greece.

Desserts

If you 'eat Greek', you rarely have room left for such effete indulgences as 'dessert'. Restaurants have a dessert menu and most tavernas have something on offer, including fresh fruit, the best way to finish a meal; or you could ask for the lip-smacking *giaourti kai meli*, yoghurt with honey. Alternatively, if in Corfu Town, move on to a *zaharoplastio*, a word which translates marvellously as 'sugar-sculptor'. This is a café-pâtisserie, where you can indulge in a feast of *kataifi* (wheat cakes soaked in honey); or *baklava* (nut and syrup cake); or *loukoumades* (fritters soaked in honey).

63

BENÍTSES ● ●

There are two Benítses: brash resort and traditional Greek village. Old Benítses is an absolute delight. Fishing caiques, laden with brightly coloured nets and floats, lie with their bows towards the little harbour quays. Across the main road from the harbour is the village square with its mix of Venetian buildings and two-storeyed houses, busy little cafés and tavernas. Two grand old pine trees lean precariously from their fractured stone bases and there are seats in a small landscaped garden where a big war memorial features the dramatic relief of an angel. A short distance north from the square, a narrow alleyway (signposted 'Roman Baths') leads between seafront houses, past an alarmingly huge satellite dish, to a lemon grove and the small but impressive ruins of the bathhouse of a Roman villa. The old village also extends inland along a narrow lane (signposted) to the right of Petros super-market. Amid the citrus trees and bougainvillaea is a fine old church with a well-head in its courtyard.

Resort Benítses lies south of the old village, beyond the tiny roadside Church of St Dimitrious with its single bell-tower and tiled roof. The resort is the hub of a busy social whirl during the summer, especially for young North Europeans seeking Mediterranean sun and fast food and fast music. The resort's reputation for all-night fun and games has mellowed in recent years, although the clubs and bars are still lively. The beach is a grudgingly narrow shingle strip with the busy main road alongside. All types of watersport are available, and you can hire sunbeds for pavement grilling if the beach is impossibly crowded.

Above: Old Benítses survives around its traditional harbour

BOÚKARIS ✪

South of Moraïtika and Mesongí the main road swings inland and then runs down the centre of the island. An alternative road south (► 70) from Messongí hugs the east coast and leads past numerous tiny roadside beaches and rocky coves before turning inland at Boúkaris. There is a small beach here which has a jetty, and a beachside taverna with thatched umbrella awnings.

A rough track continues south along the coast and can be walked or cycled for about 2km to the fishing village of Petrití, where some impressively large trawlers moor alongside small caiques in a busy working harbour.

DASIÁ (DASSIÁ) ✪

Dassiá's shingle beach is spared the roadside clamour of other resorts, but its popularity and proximity to Corfu Town makes the seafront a busy place. A zone of hotels and apartments lies between the beach and the main road which has the bulk of gift shops, tavernas and services, as well as the lavish frontages of two big hotels, the Corfu Chandris and the Dasiá Chandris. There is a popular campsite inland from the main road. The beach's shallow waters, reached down narrow lanes, make it safe for young children. Wooden jetties run seaward to cater for the excursion boats that arrive loaded with day visitors and leave for trips. All types of watersports, including water-skiing and paragliding, add to the bustle, and there are various beachfront café-bars and tavernas. The once independent resort of Dafnilia at the southern end of the bay is now merged with Dassiá.

⊞ 28B2
⊠ 23km south of Corfu Town on minor coast road from Messongí
🍴 Boúkaris Beach Taverna (€–€€)
♿ Road is level with adjoining beach
↔ Messongí (► 77)
? Roadside parking

⊞ 28B4
⊠ 13km north of Corfu Town on main road
🍴 Choice of cafés, snack bars on beach (€–€€)
🚌 Blue bus No 7 from San Rocco Square, Corfu Town–Dassiá
🚤 Excursions from beach
↔ Ipsos (► 90)
? Roadside parking

Tree-shaded Dassiá has an ideal family beach

🚩 28A6

✉ 5–15km northwest of Corfu

🍴 Mathráki: café (€); Othoní: tavernas (€), restaurant (€€); Erikoussa: beachside taverna (€)

🚢 Excursions from Sidári and from Ágios Stéfanos (northwest) daily during season, depending on sea conditions. Twice-weekly car ferry from Corfu Town. The crossing can sometimes be quite lively in these open waters

DIAPÓNTIA NISIÁ (DIAPONDÍA ISLANDS) ✪

Corfu's Diapondía Islands are the northwest outposts of Greece. The nearest, and smallest, of the three inhabited islands is Mathráki, just under 5km from the Corfu coast. The two others are Erikoussa and Othoní.

The Diapondías have a long history; flint tools of the early Stone Age, the neolithic and the Bronze Age have been discovered on all of them, and for centuries they were important refuges for ships. At times they were also probably nests of pirates. Othoní, the largest of the group, is claimed by some to be Calypso's island from which Odysseus eventually escaped, only to be shipwrecked at Érmones (► 67), on the coast of ancient Corfu.

All the islands have beaches and there are some tourist services, including a few tavernas and rooms to let – but choice is very limited. Mathráki is the handsomest of the islands, deeply wooded and with a very long beach. Othoní has several beaches including Aspri Ammos, the 'white sand', on its western shore. Erikoussa, the busiest of the three, has a long curving beach in front of its main settlement, Porto.

🚩 28A5

✉ 18km northwest of Corfu. From the Paleokastritsa road, go through village to a little car park reached down a slip road to the left

🍴 Elizabeth's Taverna (€)

🚌 Green bus from Avramiou Street, Corfu Town–Paleokastritsa, then short steep walk

🔄 Paleokastritsa (► 24)

❓ In late June there is a festival at Doukádes in celebration of St John

DOUKÁDES ✪

This archetypal Corfiot mountain village is spectacularly sited beneath limestone crags, with a steep hinterland of lovely olive groves. Viewed from the Troumbetas Pass road, the great cliff above the clustered village seems to hang in mid-air. Doukádes has a pretty central square with adjacent tavernas and shops and there are seats alongside the Church of the Blessed Virgin Mesochoritissa, notable for its splendid doorcases and doors. Numerous Venetian buildings of great style grace the village.

A local lady sits in the sunshine outside her brightly painted house in Doukádes

ÉRMONES

Picturesque Érmones Bay has a strong claim to being the place where Homer's Odysseus was washed ashore after his voyage from Calypso's isle. Here Odysseus was discovered by the beautiful Nausicaa, daughter of Alcinous, King of the Phaeacians – the legendary inhabitants of Scheria, ancient Corfu. Today, the dominant Érmones Beach Hotel has added a funicular to the scene. Its track slices down the hillside between hotel bungalows and the beach; the ultimate hotel lift, undreamt of by Homer.

Érmones lies between two steep headlands, its shingle beach lapped by turquoise water. The Rópa River runs into the bay across the middle of the beach and this feature has strengthened the Homeric associations further. Here Nausicaa and her handmaidens came to wash clothes 'in the flowing stream of the lovely river', and, while playing a form of classical beach ball, discovered the exhausted Odysseus. They took him to King Alcinous's castle, from where eventually he returned home to Ithaca.

Today, beach ball is just one of Érmones' numerous activities, which include paragliding, and there are several tavernas above the beach. The beach shelves quickly into deep water and this should be kept in mind as far as young children and poor swimmers are concerned.

A rough path leads north from the road end above the beach, along the northern arm of the bay to the little Church of Zoodochos Pighi, the Source of Life. Here there are fine views to a lonely headland.

Inland from Érmones, on the flatlands of the Rópa Valley, is the Corfu Golf and Country Club, where a meandering stream adds zest to the course.

➕ 28A4
✉ 17km from Corfu Town on west coast. Reached from Rópa Valley, through Vátos

🍴 Nausika Restaurant Bar (€–€€)
🚌 Green bus from Avramiou Street, Corfu Town–Vátos
🚢 Excursion boats to and from other resorts
↔ Glyfáda (➤ 69)
❓ Limited parking above beach

Above: *Érmones beach, legendary landing place of shipwrecked Odysseus*

➕ 28B2

✉ 25km south of Corfu Town. Reached from the main road about 1km beyond Messongí

🍴 Alonáki Beach taverna (€)

🚌 Green bus from Avramiou Street. Corfu Town–Ágios Matthéos. Get off at the Gardíki turn, then walk for 0.5km

↔ Lake Korissión (➤ 22)

❓ Very limited roadside parking by castle

GARDÍKI ✪✪

At the heart of the Gardíki area, which lies between Mount Ágios Matthéos (➤ 51) and Lake Korissión (➤ 22), stands the ruin of a Byzantine fortress, the only historic site of note in the southern half of the island. In this same area Stone Age tools have also been discovered, indicating that it was an attractive site for settlement from earliest times. Gardíki Fortress, which probably dates from the early 13th century, may have been built by the mainland Byzantines as a defence against raids by Genoese pirates, Sicilians and Venetians. The eight postern towers and connecting walls survive in a reasonable condition. There are remnants of typical Byzantine tile courses in the south tower, and the faded remnants of religious frescoes can

be made out on its upper walls. Although the interior is overgrown, a path winds its way round the outside. The fortress was one of the last outposts of the Byzantine world before Corfu fell under the influence of the Angevin rulers of Sicily, and later the Venetians.

Lake Korissión is reached by continuing from the fortress to the scattered hamlet of Gardíki, from where a side road leads to the north end of the lake. A short distance further on from the Lake Korissión turn, a track leads down to the isolated Kanouli and Alonáki beaches (➤ 76). Alonáki has several small fishing boats, which are launched down ramps and hauled up after use.

Did you know ?

In the 14th century the Angevin rulers of Corfu divided the island into four administrative regions: Gyro (The Circle) – northwest; Oros (The Mountain) – northeast; Mesis (The Centre) – the centre of the island; and Lefkímmi – the south. The names still survive, and denote different types of colourful costume worn by Corfiot women for traditional dancing.

The crumbling Byzantine stonework of Gardíki Castle

GLYFÁDA ✪✪

Glyfáda, one of the finest beaches on the west coast of Corfu, with a long stretch of golden sands, is reached down a winding road. There has been much development here and major hotels tend to dominate the backdrop of tree-covered coastal hills. Watersports of every kind are available, and these include sailing and windsurfing. The beach shelves steeply in places, but otherwise Glyfáda is the kind of sandy paradise adored by youngsters. Tavernas line the beachfront and popular venues such as the Aloha Beach bar go non-stop until late into the night. You can find some peace and quiet along tracks and paths to the north and south of the resort.

🔢 28B4
✉ 16km from Corfu Town
🍴 Beachside tavernas (€–€€)
🚌 Green Bus from Avramiou Street, Corfu Town–Vátos–Glyfáda
🚢 Excursion boats from neighbouring resorts
↔ Pélekas (► 82)
❓ Car park behind beach

Glyfáda beach on the exhilarating west coast

GOUVIÁ ✪

Gouviá (close to Corfu Town and therefore popular) lies on the shores of a deep bay between the horned promontories of Ákrotírio Komméno and Ákrotírio Tourka. Kondókali (► 74) lies at the southern end of the bay. Dominating part of the southern shoreline is the Gouviá yacht marina, which has increased the general activity at both resorts. The narrow shingle beach at Gouviá becomes crowded in summer, especially since ferries from Corfu Town bring in large numbers of day visitors. There is enough beach equipment and watersports, including paragliding, to suit all tastes, and bathing is very safe. The resort has numerous restaurants, tavernas, cafés, bars and shops, with the nightlife geared towards young people.

Gouviá Bay was used by the Venetians as a harbour and as a ship-repair and provisioning station. In 1537, and again in 1716, Turkish invaders landed here in ill-fated attempts to capture Corfu.

🔢 28B4
✉ 8km north of Corfu Town
🍴 Snack bars and tavernas (€–€€)
🚌 Blue bus 7 from San Rocco Square, Corfu Town–Kondókali–Gouviá–Dassiá
🚢 Excursion boats from Corfu Town
↔ Kondókali (► 74)
❓ Parking at south end of beach near marina

69

A Drive Around South Corfu

Distance
60km

Time
4–5 hours, with stops at the Achilleion and Benítses included

Start/end point
Corfu Town
 28C4

Lunch
Boúkari Beach taverna (£–££)
 Boúkaris

This drive passes the Achilleion then continues south through Benítses and Boúkaris before returning along a winding mountain road (minor roads may have pot-holes).

Start at the Old Port in Corfu Town. Drive west from the Old Port along Xenofondos Stratigou and Eth Antistasseos. Continue along the coast road for 3km to a big junction. Take the left turn, signposted Lefkími. Follow signs for Lefkími and Achilleío. In about 4km, at the busy Vrioni junction, keep right, signposted Achilleío. Follow Achilleío signs to reach Gastoúri and then the Achilleion itself.

The Achilleion (➤ 16) is worth visiting if you have not already done so.

Continue from the Achilleion and descend steeply through numerous bends to the coast road. Turn right and continue to Benítses.

Old Benítses (➤ 64), at the northern entrance to the resort, is a charming place to explore.

Continue south to Moraïtika. At the junction beyond the resort, where the main road bends sharply right, go straight across. In about 500m, at a T-junction, take the left turn, signposted Messongí. At the next T-junction by the supermarket, turn right and follow a narrow coastal road for 4km to Boúkaris (➤ 65). Turn sharp right and uphill between tavernas. Continue to Kouspádes. Beyond the village, keep

Did you know ?

In Corfu, as in the rest of Greece, when oncoming Greek drivers flash their lights they are indicating that they are coming ahead, not inviting you to drive on. Do not be upset if local drivers do not acknowledge you if you give way to them; they follow the very sensible dictum that someone has to give way and it may as well be you.

right at the next junction, then go downhill. At the next junction, on a right-hand bend, keep right and continue to Neohoraki. Climb steeply to reach a T-junction at Argyrádes. Turn right.

A tree-shaded refreshment break at Benítses

The farming village of Argyrádes is worth lingering at.

Continue north and, after 9km, cross a bridge. At a junction on a sharp right-hand bend, signposted Corfu and Benitses to the right, go straight across on to a narrow road. Continue to Ág Déka. Drive very carefully through the village, then descend through several steep bends. At a T-junction, go right, signposted Kérkyra, and follow signs to the town.

KALÁMI (➤ 20, TOP TEN)

KANÓNI (➤ 21, TOP TEN)

KASSIÓPI ✪✪

The old port of Kassiópi lies within a picturesque setting of wooded promontories. Today the village is a thriving resort – the main street and approach roads are crammed with cafés, bars, clubs and shops – but mixed in with all of this are important relics of its ancient past. There was a prehistoric settlement here and a Corinthian 'city' long before the Romans colonised the site. Beneath the village church lie the remains of a temple to Jupiter Cassius, from whom Kassiópi gets its name. Wealthy Romans came here for recreation, thus setting an ancient precedent for today's tourism. Amongst the visitors were Cato, Cicero and Tiberius. Even Nero passed through on his mad way to the Games at Corinth. The Romans fortified the headland above the harbour, and a castle was built in the 13th century by the Angevin rulers of Corfu. The Venetians, in their turn, wrecked this fortress and built one of their own, the broken walls of which still encircle the crown of the hill. Kassiópi's church is dedicated to the Blessed Virgin Kassiópitra, and possesses an icon of the Virgin that was credited at one time with having miraculous powers. This made the village a place of pilgrimage long before Spyrídon (➤ 14) became Corfu's patron saint.

Kassiópi is still a working fishing port and the harbour area has a lively atmosphere, especially in the mornings. The pebble beaches are small and hidden away behind headlands, whereas the larger Kalamionas Beach, and Imerolia Beach, farther north, lie alongside the main road and have various watersports on offer.

🚗 28C5
📮 37km north of Corfu Town on main coast road
🍴 Large choice of snack bars and tavernas (€–€€)
🚌 Green bus from Avramiou Street, Corfu Town–Kassiópi
⛴ Ferry boats to and from Corfu Town. Excursions to other resorts
↔ Ágios Stéfanos (northeast) (➤ 54)
❓ Parking at harbour and at north end of resort by Kalamionas Beach

Kassiópi, between blue skies and blue sea

KÁVOS ✪

Kávos is Corfu's premier resort for loud and lively holiday-making, although no one is too lively at midday thanks to late-night sessions in the numerous bars. This is emphatically a young persons' place, but its long (over 2km) sandy beach, safe bathing and varied watersports makes it popular with families, too. Old Kávos survives in the form of a handful of real fishing boats moored offshore.

Kávos has dozens of bars and clubs, and the first thing anyone who is looking for local colour will notice is the total absence of the Greek language on signs and billboards. But in anyone's language, the beach is still a great place to enjoy all that Mediterranean sun. The sand finally relents in the south, where low cliffs begin. Beyond are the lonelier reaches of Ákrotírio (Cape) Asprókavos, if you feel in need of some solitude.

+ 28C1
⊠ 45km south of Corfu Town at end of main road south
🍴 Snack-bars and tavernas (€–€€)
🚌 Green bus from Avramiou Street, Corfu Town–Kávos
🚤 Excursion boats/hire boats
♿ Few
↔ Cape Asprókavos (► 56), Lefkímmi (► 75)
❓ Limited roadside parking

Rest and recovery at Kávos with a view of mainland Greece

KÉNTROMA (KÉNDROMA) ✪

On the northeast coast between the better known resorts of Nissaki and Kalámi are a number of tiny coves with shingle beaches; they are reached down steep, narrow lanes, which are unsuitable for cars, branching off from the main road. Kéndroma lies just to the south of Agni (► 56) amid a coastal landscape of tree-covered slopes ending at rocky promontories and a sea of exquisite blues and greens.

A short distance southwest of Kéndroma is the Sol Elite Nisáki Beach Hotel, beyond which is Kamináki, another tiny cove with nothing but a shingle beach and a nearby taverna.

+ 28C5
⊠ 28km north of Corfu Town on northeast coast
🍴 Tavernas (€) at coves
🚌 Green bus from Avramiou Street, Corfu Town–Kassiópi
🚤 Excursion boats visit
↔ Kalámi (► 20), Nissaki (► 79)
❓ Parking and turning at the beaches is extremely difficult

73

KONTÓKALI (KONDÓKALI) ✪

Kondókali, the first resort to the north of Corfu Town, is fast becoming the service centre for the expanding marina that takes up the adjoining shoreline. The resort has an excellent range of restaurants, tavernas and bars. The narrow pebble beaches become crowded in summer. Extended and modernised, the marina has capacity for over 800 boats and is now equipped with most services and facilities, including car rental. It is the island's main base for yacht chartering. The bay on which Kondókali and its neighbour Gouviá stands was once used by the Venetians as a harbour and service port. At the northern end of the resort a lane, signposted 'Venetian Boatyard', leads to the shore and then turns left alongside the marina's perimeter fence. At the road end are the remains of a Venetian 'arsenal' or boat-repair yard, a striking collection of skeletal arches with faded Venetian motifs.

KOULOÚRA ✪

Kouloúra is a close neighbour to Kalámi, but has a rare sense of exclusiveness, partly because there is no beach to speak of. Excursion boats visit Kouloúra, however, and the solitary taverna is very popular. The tiny bay is set against a backdrop of poker-straight cypresses and feathery pines. Its charm is enhanced by the curve of a harbour breakwater that shelters working fishing boats, and by its focal point, the handsome house that stands on the site of an ancient fortress and retains the bell-tower of a medieval chapel. The house is private; its outlook is to the sea, its privacy secured by trees. On calm days, the Corfu Channel between here and Albania can seem like an inland lake.

✚ 28B4
✉ 7km north of Corfu Town
🍽 Restaurants and snack bars (€–€€)
🚌 Blue bus No 7, from San Rocco Square, Corfu Town–Kondókali–Gouviá–Dassiá
♿ Few
↔ Gouviá (➤ 69)
❓ Limited roadside parking

Above: the marina at Kondókali, Corfu's 'floating' village

✚ 28C5
✉ 31km north of Corfu Town
🍽 Kouloúra Taverna (€€)
🚤 Excursion boats visit
↔ Kalámi (➤ 20)
❓ Very limited parking at Kouloúra; turning is awkward

LEFKÍMMI ★★

The far south of Corfu may have Kávos as a major resort, but the true character of the area is epitomised by the town of Lefkímmi – a straggle of communities, including Melikia, Potami, Anaplades and Ringlades, that have merged into one. Lefkímmi, or 'Ta Lefki' to locals, makes a refreshing contrast to resort Corfu. It is the commercial centre of the south's farming and vine-growing area, and reflects the everyday life of the island beyond the beaches. Today, Lefkímmi is bypassed by a dual carriageway which hurtles south to Lefkímmi Port where it ends at the entrance to a vast quayside. From here ferries leave for Igoumenítsa on the mainland and for Paxoí (▶ 80–1).

Áno (Higher) Lefkímmi is the first part of the town entered from the main road when arriving from the north. By the roadside is the handsome Church of St Arsenios with domed bell-towers on either side of its arcaded façade. Arsenios (876–953) was the first Archbishop of Corfu; he was

28C1

40km south of Corfu Town

River Taverna, Potami (€)

Green bus from Avramiou Street, Corfu Town–Kávos

Few

Kávos (▶ 73)

Roadside parking. Lefkímmi Festival, 8 July

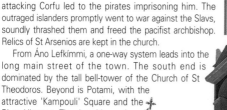

Did you know ?

Spilling wine brings good luck. But spilling oil brings bad. And money will come your way if your Greek coffee has bubbles on its surface. In the Lefkímmi region people place full bottles of wine and oil on their roofs to secure good fortune for house and occupants.

lionised when his efforts to dissuade Slav pirates from attacking Corfu led to the pirates imprisoning him. The outraged islanders promptly went to war against the Slavs, soundly thrashed them and freed the pacifist archbishop. Relics of St Arsenios are kept in the church.

From Áno Lefkímmi, a one-way system leads into the long main street of the town. The south end is dominated by the tall bell-tower of the Church of St Theodoros. Beyond is Potami, with the attractive 'Kampouli' Square and the River Himaros. The riverside roads lead south for 1.5km to the river mouth where there are small beaches and sand dunes.

LÍMNI KORISSIÓN (LAKE KORISSIÓN) (▶ 22, TOP TEN)

The twin domes of Lefkimmi's Church of St Arsenios dominate the surrounding countryside

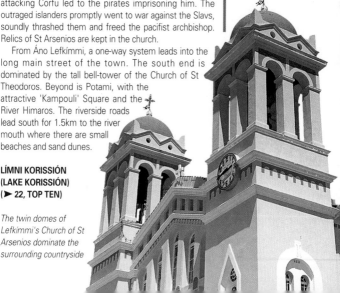

A Cycle Ride Around Southwest Corfu

Distance
30km

Time
4–5 hours, with stops

Start/end point
Moraïtika
✚ 28B2
Bikes can be hired at
Moraïtika

Lunch
Alonáki Bay Taverna (€)
✉ North of Lake Korissión
☎ (06610) 75872/76118

Donkeys are still an
essential form of
transport in Corfu

This route seeks out the less hilly parts of southern Corfu in the Lake Korissión area.

Start at the southern end of the resort of Moraïtika (➤ 78). Follow the main road west for about 1km to a junction where the road bends sharply left. Keep left and then cross a bridge. In a few metres, at a junction beside a garage, go right. Continue for 4km to reach Ágios Matthéos (➤ 51).

If you want an extra challenge, push your bike up Mount Ágios Matthéos by following a steep lane going off left at the entrance to the village.

Beyond Ágios Matthéos, go left at a junction signposted Paramonas Beach. Keep to the main road, passing a tiny roadside church. At a junction with a mass of signs, keep straight ahead. Continue past Ákrotírio (Cape) Várka and, in 3km, where the road bends left, turn off right down a rough track by a dented signpost for Kanouli Beach. Keep to the main track.

Visit Kanouli Beach if you have time.

On the main track continue in and out of olive groves, then, just beyond an avenue of big cacti plants, go right at a junction. Continue to a junction with a surfaced road and a sandy track. Turn right down the sandy track, signposted Alonáki Beach. Keep to the main track and soon reach a junction with a track going right to a taverna and the tiny Alonáki Beach, which rewards a visit. On the main route, keep ahead to reach the head of Lake Korissión (➤ 22). Follow the track south between the lake and the beach to a sea channel. Return to the head of the lake, then turn right along a sandy track. Turn left by the taverna and follow the track, then a surfaced road, to a T-junction. Turn right and continue to Gardíki Castle (➤ 68). Turn right at the junction, right again at the next junction and retrace the route to Moraïtika.

MAKRÁDES ⊗

The little village of Makrádes lies on the road north from Paleokastritsa at the junction with the lane to Kríni and the fortress of Angelókastro (▶ 18). Makrádes works very hard at being the retail hub of the known world. Roadside stalls and their insistent traders, selling everything from embroidered table linen to knitwear, ceramics and carpets, lie in wait for summer coach parties while tavernas and cafés help you to get rid of the small change.

Just before Makrádes is Lákones, the village with the view to beat all views. It stands high above Paleokastritsa at the end of a wild series of rising S-bends, with breathtaking views of the west coast.

🞧 28A5
✉ 35km northwest of Corfu Town
🍴 Cafés and tavernas (€€)
🚌 Green bus from Avramiou Street, Corfu Town–Makrádes
↔ Angelókastro (▶ 18)
❓ Roadside parking

It is just a few steps from the sunbeds to the sea at Messongí beach

MESONGÍ (MESSONGÍ) ⊗

Separated from Moraïtika by the Messongí River, Messongí is the first resort south of Corfu Town to escape from the main road. The coast sweeps away in a gentle curve to the south where tree-covered hills fill the horizon. Although the sand and shingle beach is very narrow, it has safe bathing and is ideal for families. A narrow road, packed with shops and tavernas, leads from the north end of the beach to the river bank.

South from Messongí, a coastal road (▶ 70) leads to Boúkaris (▶ 65) past a number of good fish tavernas. Apart from relaxed meals in the evenings, there is very little nightlife. For restless youth, there are the livelier attractions of nearby Moraïtika, while the clubs of Benítses are only 8km to the north.

🞧 28B2
✉ 22km south of Corfu Town
🍴 Cafés and tavernas (€–€€)
🚌 Green bus from Avramiou Street, Corfu Town–Kávos or Corfu Town–Messongí
🚢 Excursion boats to other resorts
↔ Moraïtika (▶ 78)
❓ Roadside parking

Large fishing boats, like this one moored near Moraïtika, still fish Corfu's seas

🕂 28B2

✉ 20km south of Corfu Town, on main coast road

🍽 Cafés and tavernas on beach and in main street (€–€€)

🚌 Green bus from Avramiou Street, Corfu Town–Kávos and Corfu Town–Messongí

⛵ Excursion boats from beach

↔ Benítses (➤ 64) and Messongí (➤ 77)

❓ Parking in main street

MORAÏTIKA

The name Moraïtika sounds convincingly Hawaiian and the resort does its best to live up to the image: the beach has more exotic palms and thatched umbrellas to the square metre than you can throw a Malibu board at. The only thing missing is the surf.

Like Benítses, Moraïtika is made up of old and new. Áno (Upper) Moraïtika, a delightful complex of old houses, modern villas, and a couple of tavernas, all happily swamped in bougainvillaea, is tucked away on the high ground above the north end of the resort.

The resort proper runs to the south of here, the dusty main road lined with restaurants, tavernas, bars, clubs, cafés and shops. Between road and sea is a broad swathe of land, dotted with villas and hotels, that runs down to Moraïtika's long stretch of sun-trapping sand and shingle beach. The southern end of the beach is dominated by the very large Messongí Beach Hotel, which has its own gymnasium, tennis court, swimming pools, restaurants, beach taverna, café and shopping centre. There are water-sports in plenty at Moraïtika, including gentler alternatives for children. The beach even has freshwater shower points and a changing stall at its midpoint.

MYRTIÓTISSA ✪✪

Beautiful Myrtiótissa, with its backdrop of tree-covered cliffs, was once a genuine 'Desert Island' beach, praised by Lawrence Durrell for its 'lion-gold' sand. It is now hugely popular with determined beach fanciers and can become overcrowded at the height of the season. Difficulty of access and the looming cliffs behind the beach have discouraged permanent development, however, the only blot being the line of telegraph poles and wires that lead to the little **Monastery** of the Blessed Virgin Myrtiótissa. This lies at the end of a track that runs past the solitary Bella Vista Taverna. It was founded in response to the discovery, in a myrtle bush, of an abandoned icon of the Virgin. The monastery building has very fine arched doorways and carved keystones, which contrast charmingly with the used food cans that serve as flowerpots in the forecourt.

The beach at Myrtiótissa shelves slightly and there are offshore reefs and rocks of very rough conglomerate. A makeshift snack bar operates on the beach in summer.

🚩 28A4

✉ 12km west of Corfu Town. Reached down a 1km rough track (not suitable for cars), signposted from the Glyfáda road, or by 2.5km path from the village of Vátos

🍴 Snack bar on beach (€) summer only and Myrtiótissa restaurant (€) uphill from the beach

🚌 Green bus from Avramiou Street, Corfu Town–Vátos

🚤 Excursion boats arrive from other resorts

❓ Parking at beach is very limited

Monastery

🕐 8–1, 5–8

The beautiful, remote Myrtiótissa beach on the rugged west coast

NISÁKI (NISSAKI) ✪

The coastline here, below Mount Pandokrator's steep slopes, consists of a series of tiny, rocky coves. Cafés and tavernas on the twisting main road overlook the sea, while Nissaki's main attraction, tiny, but exquisite crescents of white shingle, are reached down a surfaced lane. The luxurious Nissaki Beach Hotel, signposted from the main road, has a beach directly below it with numerous facilities that can be enjoyed by non-residents.

🚩 28C5

✉ 24km north of Corfu Town, on the main coast road

🍴 Tavernas (€€)

🚌 Green bus from Avramiou Street, Corfu Town–Kassiópi

🚤 Excursion boats from neighbouring resorts

❓ Limited parking

PALAIOKASTRÍTSA (PALEOKASTRITSA) (► 24, TOP TEN)

An Excursion to Paxoí & Antipaxoí

Paxoí (Paxos) lies 48km to the south of Corfu Town, just 11km south of Ákrotírio Asprókavos, and is a popular destination for day excursions from Corfu. It is decidedly up-market, thanks to the large number of visiting yacht crews and to Paxos devotees with a proprietorial air. Prices tend to be above the average for the Ionian as a whole, due in part to the high cost of imports.

The stylish waterfront at Gáïos on Paxos

Getting There
Ferries operate to Paxos from Corfu Town and there are cruise boats from Kávos. It is essential to make enquiries at several ferry agencies because of a complex and often changing ferry system.

Paxoí (Paxos)

The island, 11km long and 5km wide, is swathed in olive trees, pines and cypresses, giving the hilly interior a deceptively rounded look. It is a delightful place, where life is measured at a much slower pace than on Corfu. Dusty tracks wind through the olive groves to small settlements or to remote coves and pebble beaches – although Paxos is not a beach-lover's paradise. The south and west coasts of the island are spectacular, with steep cliffs, huge, cathedral-like sea caves and wind-sculpted rock formations, such as the stupendous pinnacle of Tripitos, linked by an arch to the south coast. The limestone of the cliffs glows pink and ochre in the setting sun.

The Venetians oversaw the 15th-century transformation of Paxos into one enormous olive grove, and the Paxíots created an almost formal landscape of terraces and drystone walling that survives (albeit neglected in some places) today. The Venetian influence is seen also in the buildings of the island's principal port, Gáïos, and in tiny hamlets and numerous scattered ruins. Offshore from Gáïos is the tree-covered island of St Nicholas, complete with its ruins of a 15th-century Venetian fortress. The smaller Panagia Islet has an old church and a lighthouse.

Gáïos has a lively little harbourside *plateía* with streets and alleyways radiating from it.

The two other main settlements are Lákka at the northern tip of the island, and Longos, on the east coast, midway between Gáïos and Lákka. Buses operate between all three, but exploring the island on foot is a rewarding option, although you need more than a day visit to get the best from this Ionian jewel.

Antipaxoí (Antipaxos)

Antipaxos is only a few kilometres from Paxos and can be reached from Gáïos by fast ferry boat. A mere 3sq km in size, the island is a complex of tracks and paths through olive and vine-growing country, a place where some kind of solitude can be found even at the height of summer. The east coast beaches at Vrika, Mesovrika and Voutoumi are attractive, although they tend to become crowded with day visitors. There are enough tavernas to cater for daytime needs.

A typical Paxos beach where the sea and sky always seem more blue

Did you know ?

Mythical Paxos is said to have been severed from the southern tip of Corfu by one blow of the sea god Poseidon's trident (now the emblem of Paxos). Poseidon then dragged the new island far enough south to make of it an idyllic retreat for himself and his lady, Amphitriti, thus setting a precedent for exclusiveness.

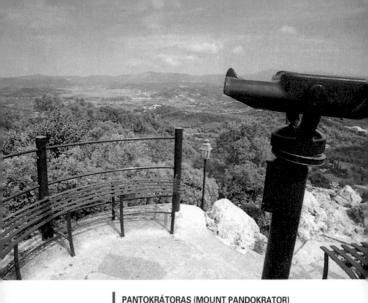

PANTOKRÁTORAS (MOUNT PANDOKRATOR)
(► 26, TOP TEN)

PÉLEKAS ⚫⚫

This hilltop village has evolved into something of an inland tourist resort due to the popularity of nearby Glyfáda on the coast and of small beaches, such as Kontoyialos and Gialiskari, which can be reached down steep lanes and tracks. Above the village, a famous viewpoint, known variously as the Kaiser's Lookout, Tower or Throne, has added to the busy trail of summer visitors. It was to this hilltop that Kaiser Wilhelm II motored frequently from the Achilleion Palace (► 16) to admire the spectacular sunsets off the west coast. The viewpoint is reached by following a steep road signposted from the centre of Pélekas. Just before the summit, the road passes between the tiny whitewashed Church of the Virgin of the Annunciation and its bell-tower. There is parking at the road end, from where a paved path leads under a little archway and on through trees to the circular viewpoint with its railing and seats. The views are spectacular; east to Corfu Town and Vídos Island; northwest along the green trough of the Rópa Valley; south to Mount Ágios Matthéos; and west across a green wooded landscape to the western sea. Bring your own binoculars; the mounted pair at the lookout do not work.

Pélekas itself retains the charm of a typical Corfiot hill village, although development has begun to erode its traditional character. There are several tavernas and cafés, plus numerous shops and tourist agencies. In the central square, with its war memorial and well-kept church, an old sea mine, now painted blue and white, serves as an eccentric plant pot.

➕ 28B4

✉ 13km from Corfu Town on west coast

🍴 Jimmy's (€€)

🚌 Blue bus No 11 from San Rocco Square, Corfu Town–Pélekas

↔ Glyfáda (► 69)

❓ Limited parking in village. Parking at viewpoint

Above: *spectacular views can be had from 'Kaiser's Lookout' above the village of Pélekas*

A Walk on the Northeast Coast

The route leads from the undeveloped Paralía Avláki (Avláki Beach) uphill through olive groves, then returns by way of a broad track.

Start at the west end of Avláki Beach. Follow the road up from the beach for about 50m and where it bends sharply right, go left up a rough track. In 30m, at a junction, go left. In 100m, at the next junction, go left and climb steeply to pass between houses and farm buildings.

Dogs may bark fiercely here, but it is what they have been trained to do and they are usually well-tethered. This is typical olive-growing country, where Corfiot farmers continue a centuries-old tradition begun by the Venetians. Please respect the farmers' privacy.

The track levels off beyond the buildings and continues through olive groves. Pass a little white building and a circular stone water tank on the right, and keep climbing steadily.

Note the black olive nets rolled up under the trees. These are stretched out beneath the branches during the winter to catch the falling fruit. (The notices pinned to trees here translate as 'Hunting is prohibited'.)

Pass an attractive little building with an arched doorway. Reach a final rise alongside a fenced and gated enclosure, then pass a junction with another track coming in from the left. Continue to the road and turn left. In about 1km turn left on to a rough track. (The surfaced road leads in another 0.5km to Ágios Stéfanos, ▶ 54.) On the main route, follow the rough track downhill to the beach at Avláki. Follow the edge of the beach back to the start of the walk.

The rolling landscape is dotted with gnarled and twisted olive trees

Distance
6km (7km if Ágios Stéfanos is included)

Time
2 hours (3 hours if Ágios Stéfanos is included)

Start/end point
Avláki Beach
✚ 28C5

Lunch
Cavo Barbaro Taverna (€–€€); Avláki Taverna (€–€€)
✉ Avláki Beach

83

PÉRAMA

Lying on a steep, wooded shoreline beyond the busy suburb of Vrioni, but not out of earshot of the airport across the adjoining Chalkiopoúlou lagoon, Pérama is the first resort to the south of Corfu Town. Shingle beaches are reached down steep steps from the main road and, in spite of their small size, offer all sorts of facilities and most watersports. Pérama has numerous hotels, bars and gift shops and is well placed for regular bus connections, south to Benítses and beyond, and north to Corfu Town. The Achilleion (➤ 16) and the charming Gastoúri village are only 3km inland to the south.

About 2km south on the coast road are the remains of the 'Kaiser's Bridge', an elaborate pierhead built by Kaiser Wilhelm II to facilitate landing from the imperial yacht.

PERÍTHEIA (OLD PERÍTHIA)

In the hidden hollows of Mount Pandokrator's upper slopes lie the ruins of old farmsteads and villages. They were established originally by Corfu's Byzantine peoples fleeing repeated pirate raids on their coastal settlements. Abandoned villages can also be found at Old Siniés and at Rou on the east side of the mountain, but Perithia is the most impressive. Today it is being brought back to life as the shells of houses are being refurbished, and summer tavernas cater for visitors.

Perithia can be reached by the mountain road from Néa (New) Perithia, which lies on the coast road between Kassiópi and Acharávi. About 5km along this mountain road from Néa Perithia, a rough track leads off left from a steep right-hand bend on the surfaced road. (This track eventually joins the road from Strinýlas to the summit of Mount Pandokrator). For Old Perithia, keep on the surfaced road to an old church at the entrance to the village, where there is limited parking.

The framework of Perithia survives within its setting of terraced fields and scattered stands of cherry, almond, oak and walnut trees. Empty houses, complete with outside staircases and the stone brackets of missing balconies, retain their shutters and tiled roofs. But doors and windows gape, and floorboards sag alarmingly; it is dangerous to enter. At the heart of the village a cobbled lane descends to the central square, where there are two summer tavernas.

Orthodox church at the entrance to the haunting village of Old Perithia

Above: *the Church of Agii Saranda (the Forty Saints) at Perivóli*
Left: *the spirit of old Corfu survives in Perivóli*

PERIVÓLI ⊗

This is another of Corfu's down-to-earth farming villages, with its narrow lanes and alleyways, on the main road south. The church here is called Agii Saranda, the Forty Saints. The name is shared with the Albanian port of Agii Saranda, dedicated in honour of 40 Christian soldiers martyred for their faith in the 4th century by being thrown into a freezing lake.

Perivóli has a number of very traditional *kafenions* and tavernas which only aficionados of Greek living will feel at ease in. The village is the gateway to several accessible points on the great sweep of beach that runs down the southwest coast. These include Paralía Gardénos (Vitaládes Beach) reached through the village of Vitaládes and Paralía Agías Varváras (Santa Barbara Beach), also with beachside tavernas.

🔲 28C1

✉ 35km south of Corfu Town, on main road south to Lefkímmi and Kávos

🍴 Tavernas at Vitaládes Beach and at Santa Barbara Beach (€)

🚌 Green bus from Avramiou Street, Corfu Town

↔ Lefkímmi (► 75)

❓ Limited roadside parking. Some parking at beaches

85

PEROULÁDES

Corfu's northwestern limits are marked by the dramatic white cliffs of Ákrotírio (Cape) Drástis, near the village of Perouládes, which rise sheer from the sea to heights of over 50m in places. Long, narrow fins of rock jut out from the shore and gentler promontories, patched with scrub, mark the far points of land. From the village square, complete with old water pump, a narrow road runs west between huddled buildings. A few metres along the road a lane runs steeply uphill to the right, leading past the village school and church and on to Ákrotírio Drástis. Although the lane is surfaced at first, it soon becomes very rough, and driving along it is not advised. The track leads in about 1.5km to a dramatic viewpoint overlooking the Diapondía Islands (▶ 66) to the northwest. The narrow road at Perouládes leads through the village to a right turning, signposted Longas Beach. This leads shortly to the Sunset View Taverna, from where concrete steps descend to a narrow beach below towering cliffs.

A typical village house at Perouládes

Sidebar (Perouládes):

- 28A6
- 45km from Corfu Town on northwest coast
- Sunset Taverna (€€)
- Green bus from Avramiou Street, Corfu Town–Sidári–Perouládes–Ágios Stéfanos
- Sidári (▶ 88)
- Limited parking in village. Parking above Longas Beach

RÓDA

North coast Róda is a pleasant resort with safe bathing and a handful of tavernas and clubs. The main road passes some distance inland from the beach, and between the two, intensive hotel and villa development has taken place over the past few years. A little harbour within a rough breakwater marks the original fishing village, and fishing caiques still work from here. Róda's beach, narrow and sandy, with rocky patches, is backed by tavernas, cafés, gift shops and clubs. Part way up the main street is the Church of Ágios Geórgios, set in an attractive square dotted with lemon trees and plane trees. On the inland side of the main road towards Acharávi (▶ 49) are the remains of a 5th-century Doric temple to Apollo.

Sidebar (Róda):

- 28B6
- On north coast, 37km north of Corfu Town
- Cafés and tavernas (€–€€)
- Green bus from Avramiou Street, Corfu Town–Róda
- Seafront road alongside beach
- Sidári (▶ 88)
- Limited parking at seafront

A Drive Around the Northwest

A drive to the famous resort of Paleokastritsa, followed by a climb over the mountains to Sidári (➤ 88). The return to Corfu Town is via the scenic Troumbetas Pass.

Start at the Old Port in Corfu Town.
Drive west along the coast road for 3km to a big junction, and turn right. Follow signs for Paleokastritsa.

Visit Paleokastritsa (➤ 24).

Return from Paleokastritsa, and at the junction by the Paleo Club, turn sharp left uphill, signposted Lákones. Climb through a succession of hairpin bends to Lákones.

The route passes several restaurants with spectacular views from their roadside terraces.

Reach Makrádes. (Go left through Kríni to visit the hilltop fortress ruin of Angelókastro, ➤ 18.) On the main route, leave Makrádes, keeping right at junctions. Pass through Vístonas and continue for 7km to Troumbetas. Turn left here and descend through several big hairpins, then, at a junction on a right-hand bend, go left, signposted Sidári and Aríllas. Continue to a big junction and keep ahead into Sidári.

Sidári has enough beach attractions, cafés, tavernas, and shops to keep everyone happy.

Return to the big junction and go left. At the entrance to Róda, turn right at a junction, signposted Kérkyra (Corfu Town). Keep right at the next junction. Follow the main road for about 12km, keeping left at big junctions and climbing through S-bends to reach Troumbetas. Continue downhill through S-bends to the junction with the Paleokastritsa road. Turn left for Corfu Town.

Distance
105km

Time
6–7 hours, with stops

Start/end point
Old Port, Corfu Town
✚ 28C4

Lunch
Bella Vista (€–€€)
✉ On road to Lákones

Superb views of Paleokastritsa from the Lákones mountain road

🔲 28A6

✉ 36km from Corfu Town on north coast

🍴 Cafés and tavernas (€–€€)

🚌 Green bus from Avramiou Street, Corfu Town–Róda–Sidári

🚢 Excursions by boat to Kassiópi, Paleokastritsa and the Diapondía Islands, sea conditions permitting

♿ Flat access to Megali Beach. Flat access to edge of official Canal d'Amour Beach

↔ Peroulādes(➤ 86), Róda (➤ 86)

🅿 Parking at Megali Beach

Above: *the flower-fringed St Nicholas's Church at Sidári*

SIDÁRI

There are a number of good beaches at Sidári, including the large Megali Beach at the southern entrance to the resort and the smaller Canal d'Amour beaches below the sculpted sandstone cliffs of Sidári's north-facing coast. There is shallow water and safe bathing here, with every beachside facility to hand; watersports in plenty, a big water slide, go-karts, and numerous restaurants, tavernas, bars and clubs.

Halfway along the long main street is a little village square, a brave fragment of old Sidári amid the glare of tourism. Here, beneath plane trees that have their trunks painted white to guard against disease, are little seats, a seahorse fountain, and a bandstand wreathed in bougainvillaea and geraniums. On the north side of the square is the cream and white Church of St Nicholas, its porch hung with lamps and with an icon painted on its domed interior.

At the northern end of the main street a bridge crosses the Loxida River and the road beyond runs west past villas and hotels. Lanes between the buildings on the north side lead to beaches which all claim to be the location of the famous Canal d'Amour. The image of this 'Channel of Love' has worn as thin as the original sea arch that gave rise to the name and which has long since collapsed. Tradition claimed that if you swam through the original arch, various romantic events would result. Today, the official Canal d'Amour is said to be an eroded inlet at the most easterly beach on the north-facing coast. On the other hand, some say it is the channel between a pair of sea stacks further west, where the little beaches of Vithismeno, Apotripiti and Atri vie for attention.

Above: *sandstone outcrop at a Sidári beach*
Left: *the decorated entrance dome of St Nicholas's Church at Sidári*

Well-worn steps lead to the fascinating folklore museum in the village of Sinarádes

<table>
<tr><td>✚</td><td>28B3</td></tr>
<tr><td>✉</td><td>15km from Corfu Town on the west coast</td></tr>
<tr><td>🍴</td><td>Cafés and tavernas (€–€€)</td></tr>
<tr><td>🚌</td><td>Green bus from Avramiou Street, Corfu Town–Sinarádes–Ágios Górdis</td></tr>
<tr><td>♿</td><td>None</td></tr>
<tr><td>↔</td><td>Ágios Górdis (➤ 51)</td></tr>
</table>

Folklore Museum of Central Corfu

<table>
<tr><td>🕐</td><td>All year Tue–Sun 9:30–2. Opening hours are flexible</td></tr>
<tr><td>♿</td><td>None</td></tr>
<tr><td>👋</td><td>Cheap</td></tr>
</table>

<table>
<tr><td>✚</td><td>28B5</td></tr>
<tr><td>✉</td><td>15km north of Corfu Town on the coast road</td></tr>
<tr><td>🍴</td><td>Cafés and tavernas (€–€€)</td></tr>
<tr><td>🚌</td><td>Green bus from Avramiou Street, Corfu–Pyrgi–Ipsos</td></tr>
<tr><td>🚤</td><td>Small boats for hire and excursion boats</td></tr>
<tr><td>♿</td><td>Few</td></tr>
<tr><td>↔</td><td>Barmbáti (➤ 61), Dassiá (➤ 65)</td></tr>
<tr><td></td><td>Limited parking</td></tr>
</table>

SINARÁDES ⭐⭐

This is another traditional Corfiot village, part Venetian, part Byzantine, and with an authentic flavour of everyday island life. In the main street there is a medieval bell-tower of unpainted stone, its twin bells still in place. The village square is attractive, with huge palm trees, a small bandstand and a fountain featuring statues of rearing horses. Sinarádes has its own Philharmonic Orchestra and the square is the focus of some excellent local festivals.

A short distance along the main street south from the square is the Church of St Nicholas. Opposite, a signpost points the way up a paved alley to the delightful **Folklore Museum of Central Corfu**, a two-storeyed building reached by a narrow stairway. Part of the building is a reconstruction of a 19th-century village house with furnishings and utensils. Exhibits include farming tools, musical instruments and traditional costumes.

ÝPSOS (IPSOS)/PYRGI ⭐

The resorts of Ipsos and Pyrgi are at the heart of Corfu's so-called 'Golden Mile', and are deservedly popular because of it. They are effectively merged by a long main strip of cafés, restaurants, tavernas, bars, discos and shops on the inland side of the busy main road that skirts Ipsos Bay. An attractive harbour marks the southern end of the resort, and the rugged slopes of Mount Pandokrator make a handsome backdrop. Favoured by the young, the resort is a lively place with a reputation for all-night clubbing. However, the facilities and the safe bathing also make it a good beach for families with young children.

Where To...

Above: *there is colour everywhere on the island*
Right: *carnival time in Corfu*

91

Corfu Town

Prices

Approximate prices for a full meal with a glass of wine:

€ = **under €12**
€€ = **€12–€20**
€€€ = **over €20**

Booking Meals

Booking for town restaurants and for the more sophisticated and popular resort restaurants is advisable in high season.

For most beach-side and village tavernas, booking by phone is often irrelevant. The owners pack you in with gusto and good humour. If a taverna is full, extra tables and chairs may simply be added to garden, yard or village square. Squeeze in, tuck in, and enjoy it...

Eating Places

There are some fine distinctions between eating places in Greece. An *estiatorio* is a restaurant offering international cuisine; a taverna serves traditional Greek food; a *psistaria* is a spit-roast and chargrill taverna; a *psarotaverna* is a fish taverna; a *kafenio* is a village café; a *zaharoplastio* is a café-pâtisserie. On Corfu, the difference between a restaurant and a taverna is that the former has more sophisticated service with a wider menu, and is more likely to be found in Corfu Town. Tavernas are far more informal and dominate the scene in resorts and villages.

Aegli (€€–€€€)

A classic Liston restaurant. Eat underneath the arches or on the Esplanade, beneath the trees. Good Corfiot *tiss katsarolass* (casseroled food) and choice of international dishes.

✉ 23 Kapodistrias
☎ (06610) 31949
🕐 Lunch and dinner

Arpi (€€)

Greek country cooking comes to town: even the bread is oven-baked. Start with fasolata (bean soup), then try the cockerel *pastitsada*, or *soopi-ess* (cuttlefish). Good Greek Cabernet to go with it.

✉ Panayioti Giotopoulou (off Town Hall Square) ☎ (06610) 27715 🕐 Lunch and dinner

Art Gallery Café (€)

Pleasantly fashionable café-bar adjoining the Municipal Art Gallery. Good place to kick off an evening with drinks.

✉ Palace of St Michael and St George, East Wing, Esplanade
🕐 All day

Café Banca (€€)

Good selection of tasty snacks and range of drinks at heart of busy San Rocco Square area.

✉ 42b Alexandras Avenue (off San Rocco Square)
☎ (06610) 43290

Campiello Crêperie (€)

Good crêperie in quiet part of the Old Town. Large selection of crêpes and fine wines.

✉ 25 Petridou
☎ (06610) 23517 🕐 Dinner

Chambor (€€€)

Corfiot specialities include *bourdetto* (fish in tomato and garlic sauce).

✉ Guilford 71 ☎ (06610) 39031 🕐 Daily 9AM–2AM

Chrisomallis (€)

Traditional family-run in-town taverna. Corfiot food – *pastitsada, stifado, sofrito, moussaká* and grilled meats. Popular with locals and excellent value.

✉ 6 Nikifouro Theotoki (behind the Liston)
☎ (06610) 30342 🕐 All day

Christa's Crêperie (€)

In great location just up from Filarmonikis. Delicious selection and intimate atmosphere.

✉ Sophocleous Dousmani
☎ (06610) 40227
🕐 Lunch and dinner. Dinner only in winter

La Cucina (€€)

Italian restaurant specializing in homemade fresh pasta, served with seafood, smoked salmon or proscuitto. Excellent pizzas too.

✉ 15 Guilford Street, Porta Remounda ☎ (06610) 45029
🕐 Lunch and dinner

La Famiglia (€)

Full-blooded Italian café-restaurant. Linguine with *vorgole* (mussels); lasagne, including a vegetarian version; canelloni; *polenta con pancetta*. Imaginative desserts.

✉ 30 Maniarizi Arlioti
☎ (06610) 30270 🕐 All day

Il Giardino (€€–€€€)

Very classy Italian restaurant offering Tuscan cuisine and fine wines.

✉ 4b Vraila. Opposite the Archaeological Museum
☎ (06610) 30723 🕐 Dinner

K@feOnLine (€)
Friendly internet café where you can catch up on your email free of charge. Coffee and drinks served until 1AM.
✉ **28 Kapodistriou Street** ☎ **(06610) 46226, www.corfu-net.gr/online** 🕐 **10AM–1AM**

Kochlias (€€)
Liston bar-café. Variety of coffees, fresh fruit juices, ouzo, wines, beers, *mezes*, sandwiches, and ice-cream.
✉ **The Liston** ☎ **(06610) 28188** 🕐 **All day**

Mezedakia (€€)
A large selection of *mezes* and wines.
✉ **The Strip, 38–40 Eth Antistasseos** ☎ **(06610) 24931** 🕐 **Lunch and dinner**

Mr Pizza (€)
Suitably Italian pizzas and pastas for the Venetian part of Corfu town.
✉ **41 Prosalenti, Old Port** ☎ **(06610) 34321** 🕐 **Lunch and dinner**

Old Fortress Café (€)
At the top of the Old Fortress, with fine views of Garítsa Bay. Pastas and salads served all day. Popular spot by night.
✉ **Old Fortress, Spianáda (Esplanade)** ☎ **(06610) 48550** 🕐 **Daily 9AM–2AM**

Il Pollo (€)
South of town in Garítsa by tree-lined park. Cheery, pleasant atmosphere for traditional Corfiot dishes and grills. Large selection of *mezes*. Listen to *Cantades*, the Italian-based guitar and mandolin music of the Ionian Islands.
✉ **71 Mitr Athanassiou** 🕐 **Dinner**

Porta Remounda (€–€€)
Very good *psarotaverna* (fish taverna). Try *bourdeto*, a variety of small fish in a rich tomato-based sauce; or *soopi-ess* (cuttlefish).
✉ **14 Moustoxidi Street, off Kapodistrias** ☎ **(06610) 48661** 🕐 **Lunch and dinner**

Remezzo (€)
Just in case you missed eating *Ameriki* (American), for a change try Hambo's range of burgers and snacks. Salad bar and traditional Greek menu are also available.
✉ **San Rocco Square** ☎ **(06610) 23675**

Rex (€€–€€€)
Behind the Liston, a long-established restaurant popular with Corfiots. Adventurous sauces, including a truly local speciality, chicken in kumquat sauce. Another favourite is *xsifhia bourdetto* (swordfish in tomato and cayenne pepper sauce). Good selection of Greek wines.
✉ **66 Kapodistrias** ☎ **(06610) 39649** 🕐 **Lunch and dinner**

Tenedos (€–€€)
Eat Greek, drink Greek; enjoy guitar music in the old Spilia district, near the New Fortress. International menu as well.
✉ **1st parodos Solomou, Spilia (Tenedos)** ☎ **(06610) 36277** 🕐 **All day**

Venetian Well (€€–€€€)
At the Italianate heart of the Old Town. Remarkable international menu spanning East and West plus Greek specialities and delicious home-made desserts.
✉ **Kremásti Square** ☎ **(06610) 44761** 🕐 **Lunch and dinner. Closed Sun**

Vegetarian Options
Vegetarians may have difficulty in finding non-meat dishes in traditional tavernas. But, as so many *mezes* (starters) are vegetable only, one can often make a meal of them alone. Try *spanokeftede*s (spinach balls), *manitaria* (mushrooms), *dolmadakia* (vine leaves stuffed with rice), *saganaki* cheese fried in oil, and feta cheese. Be careful with 'mixed' dishes such as pasta with vegetables, or vegetable casserole, as small pieces of meat are often mixed in regardless.

Around the Island

Coffee

The Greeks know well that coffee-drinking makes philosophers or gossips of us all. For the safe, familiar stuff, 'Nescafé' is universally recognised as meaning instant coffee. Try *kafes Ellenika*, Greek coffee, made from thick grounds, served in tiny cups, either *sketo* (unsweetened), *metrio* (medium sweet), or *gliko* (sweetened). Do not swallow in one gulp. Sip gently. It comes with a glass of water, which can be added in small portions to settle the grounds. Try too, *kafes frappe*, a long glass of smooth, iced coffee, sweetened or unsweetened, again accompanied by a glass of water.

Acharávi
La Fattoria (€)
Excellent pizzas cooked in a traditional oven. Also full range of Italian dishes.

✉ **On main road near the roundabout** 🕓 **All day**

Maistro (€)
A lovely beachside setting for a wide-ranging traditional menu; fish specialities, local Corfiot dishes and crêpes.

✉ **Overlooking the middle of the beach** ☎ **(06630) 63020** 🕓 **Lunch and dinner**

Ágios Geórgios (Southwest)
Restaurant Panorama (€€)
Friendly family staff serve up excellent Greek specialities, including the best *kleftiko* (baked lamb) you'll ever taste.

✉ **At the coast near the centre of the resort** ☎ **(06620) 52352** 🕓 **Lunch and dinner**

Ágios Górdis
Sea Breeze (€€)
In a lovely location with terraces overlooking the beach. Features regular Greek nights including music,dancers and jugglers, and you can join in with the plate smashing. Children's play area and a good fun atmosphere.

✉ **Towards the southern end of the beach** ☎ **(06610) 53214** 🕓 **Lunch and dinner**

Ágios Spyrídonas (Ágios Spyrídon)
Ágios Spiridon Taverna (€)
In a superb setting at the southern end of this charming beach. Enjoy a big selection of *mezes* followed by traditional Greek dishes.

✉ **At the south end of the beach where the road bears north** 🕓 **Lunch and dinner**

Ágios Stéfanos (Northeast)
Cochili Taverna (€€)
A delightful harbour-front setting where you can enjoy good traditional home cooking.

✉ **Overlooking the small central beach** ☎ **(06630) 81522** 🕓 **Lunch and dinner**

Eucalyptus (€€)
Beside the shingle beach, the Eucalyptus offers good international cuisine in a great setting.

✉ **On the north side of the bay where the approach road turns south** ☎ **(06630) 82007** 🕓 **Lunch and dinner**

Ágios Stéfanos (Northwest)
Taverna O Manthos (€)
Dine out overlooking the beach from the garden restaurant. Corfiot specialities and barbecue food.

✉ **At the north end of the seafront near the jetty** ☎ **(06630) 51712** 🕓 **Lunch and dinner**

Agni
Taverna Agni (€€)
Popular and friendly beachside eating place, family run (Corfiot and English) and with marvellous local cuisine. Try anchovy fillets marinated in herb-infused olive oil and aubergine slices rolled round feta chees and baked in a tasty sauce. Main dishes include lamb casseroled in red wine and chicken cooked in champagne.

✉ **Overlooking Agni beach** ☎ **(06630) 91142** 🕓 **Lunch and dinner**

Taverna Nikolas (€€)
The most traditional of Agni's

beach tavernas, set up over 35 years ago. It has a picturesque location, very relaxing atmosphere (Pericles is the perfect Greek host and speaks excellent English) and good Greek food. Very popular with English tourists. Greek dancing some evenings.

✉ **On the beach** ☎ **(06630) 91243** 🕐 **Lunch and dinner**

Toula's (€€)

Yet another first-class taverna at Agni. Beach-side eating with classic fish dishes as well as meat. Try fish *mezes* for starters, including anchovies marinated in vinegar and lemon juice. Follow with prawn pilaff.

✉ **Overlooks beach at road end** ☎ **(06630) 91350** 🕐 **Lunch and dinner**

Alonáki

Alonáki Bay Taverna (€)

One of the most attractive and popular west coast tavernas. Homely, with tree-shaded views to the sea. Good Corfiot home cooking, fresh fish and potent local wine.

✉ **Just north of Lake Korissión, on a rough track** ☎ **(06610) 75872/76118** 🕐 **Lunch and dinner**

Áno Korakiána

Taverna Luna D'Argento (€€)

Popular all-in experience, with great traditional food accompanied by Greek dancing and – a splash of exotica – belly dancing.

✉ **In village** ☎ **(06630) 22531 (booking advised)** 🕐 **Dinner**

Benítses

Paxinos (€€)

Traditional Corfiot casserole dishes and locally caught fish. Popular with locals.

✉ **Harbour Square in the old village** ☎ **(06610) 72339** 🕐 **Lunch and dinner**

Dasiá (Dassiá)

Greco (€€€)

Good selection of traditional Greek food supplemented with French cuisine. Dancing.

✉ **Dafnilia, at south end of Dassiá** ☎ **(06610) 91765** 🕐 **Lunch and dinner**

Érmones

Érmones Beach Hotel (€€)

Sample the hotel's funicular railway and enjoy seafood and other Corfiot dishes in the hotel restaurant.

✉ **On north side of river, overlooking beach** ☎ **(06610) 94241** 🕐 **Lunch and dinner**

Nausika Restaurant Bar (€)

Great sunsets, great traditional food and live music. Try king prawns in garlic.

✉ **On south side of river, overlooking beach** 🕐 **Lunch and dinner**

Glyfáda

Aloha Beach Bar (€)

More of a music bar but with a restaurant offering breakfast, lunch and *mezes* in the evening.

✉ **Immediately south of entrance to beach** ☎ **(06610) 94380** 🕐 **10AM until late evening**

Gorgona (€)

Popular eating place with a pool. Corfiot and Greek cooking, plus charcoal grills.

✉ **Beach-side venue** ☎ **(06610) 94336** 🕐 **Lunch and dinner**

Gouviá

Filippas (€€)

Long-standing restaurant with good casserole cooking and charcoal grills. Live music at times.

✉ **Main street** ☎ **(06610) 91335/91612** 🕐 **Dinner**

Imerolia

Cavo Barbera (€€)

Just clear of busy Kassiópi. Dine in an attractive garden setting by the sea.

Non-alcoholic Drinks

You can certainly ask for tea (*tsa-i*), but try breaking the habit of a lifetime. If tea is available, make it clear if you want milk (*gala*), or sugar (*zahari*), with it. Orange juice in the best cafés is made from fresh oranges, and is delicious. Soft drinks (*anapsiktika*), are available in universal brands. Greek soft drinks, such as *portokalada* (fizzy orange), and lemon-flavoured *lemonada* are very sweet.

Ginger Beer

Ginger beer, or *tsin tsin birra*, to give it the proper Corfiot name, is still available on Corfu and can be bought in the Liston cafés. A legacy of the British protectorate, the drink is made in traditional fashion using the finest ingredients of grated ginger, lemon juice, lemon oil, water and sugar. The mix is brewed in large cauldrons and is best taken fresh, although, traditionally, it was stored for long periods in stone bottles that were sealed with little glass marble stoppers and kept in the cool waters of island wells.

Traditional Corfiot cooking features on the menu.

✉ **A few hundred metres along main road to northeast of Kassiópi** 🕓 **Dinner**

Ipsos (Ypsos)
Viceroy Indian (€–€€)

The first Indian restaurant on Corfu. Very authentic, with wide-ranging menu and proper Tandoori oven-cooking.

✉ **At north end of resort, near turn off to old Venetian boatyard** ☎ **(06610) 93814** 🕓 **Dinner. Closed Mon**

Kalámi
Pepes Taverna (€€)

Pepes is a traditional, family-run taverna offering good Corfiot and fresh fish dishes. Greek dancing at weekends.

✉ **At centre of village** ☎ **(06630) 91180** 🕓 **Lunch and dinner**

The White House (€€)

Popular for fish, sea views and literary connections: Lawrence Durrell lived here in 1937–8 and wrote his pastoral idyll, *Prospero's Cell*.

✉ **On south side of the bay** ☎ **(06630) 91251** 🕓 **Lunch and dinner**

Kamináki
Spiro's (€–€€)

Corfiot-style home cooking served in a superb beach setting.

✉ **Overlooks beach, at road end** ☎ **(06630) 91211** 🕓 **Lunch and dinner**

Kanóni
Captain's (€–€€)

Old-time favourite, with friendly owner 'Captain' George. Authentic Greek dishes are served with flair; generous helpings. Try the *kopanisti* (peppered cheese) and the *gigantes* (beans in sauce). Good *pastitsada* and *souvlaki*.

✉ **Just past the viewpoint area** 🕓 **All day**

Nafsika (€€)

Classy food, from lavish Greek dishes to chicken curry or pork fillet with mustard. Equally lavish desserts include chocolate mousse and cheesecake, as well as Greek favourites such as *baklava* and *kataifi*. Good wine list.

✉ **11 Nafsikas, opposite Divani Hotel** ☎ **(06610) 44354** 🕓 **Dinner**

Kassiópi
Janis (€–€€)

Good seafront location for this friendly and well-run restaurant. Wide-ranging menu offers excellent value. Good wine list and helpful menu for youngsters.

✉ **Kassiópi** ☎ **(06630) 81082** 🕓 **Lunch and dinner**

Three Brothers Taverna (€–€€)

Long-established and popular venue with a great selection of Corfiot dishes.

✉ **On harbour front** ☎ **(06630) 81211** 🕓 **Lunch and dinner**

Kinopiastes
Gloupos (€€)

Typical Greek fare is found here: taramosolata, crispy cheese pies, succulent spit-roasts, charcoal-grilled meats, *stifado* and *sofrito*. There is occasional evening entertainment and Greek dancing.

✉ **5 miles from Corfu Town** ☎ **(06610) 56283, 56545** 🕓 **Lunch and dinner**

Tripa Taverna (€€)

Popular venue where famous past guests include François Mitterand, Aristotle Onassis and Jane Fonda, though not necessarily together. Good selection of *mezes*. Then try spit-roasted lamb or *kleftiko* (beef baked in parchment to seal in the juices). Good desserts and house wine.

 Village is just off road from Corfu Town to Sinarádes
☎ (06610) 56333 ⏰ Dinner

Kontókali (Kondókali)
Takis (€€)
Great selection of interesting dishes. Spit roasts, grills and casseroles. Try the prawn *giouvetsi* (prawns in a sauce of tomatoes, olive oil, and parsley), topped with feta cheese).
✉ Kondókali
☎ (06610) 91259 ⏰ Dinner

Kouloúra
Kouloúra Taverna (€€)
Unbeatable setting in beautiful, unspoilt bay. Straightforward Corfiot fish dishes using fresh locally caught fish. Can get very busy at lunchtimes.
✉ On harbourside at road end
☎ (06610) 91253
⏰ Lunch and dinner

Lákones
Golden Fox (€€)
Stunning setting overlooking Paleokastritsa with views down to the coast. International menu, also a snack bar and swimming pool.
✉ On the road to Makrádes
☎ (06630) 49101/2
⏰ Lunch and dinner

Paleokastritsa
Chez George (€€)
Convenient beach-side venue. Good range of seafood, including lobster and mullet dishes.
✉ At end of main beach, by roadside, opposite car park
☎ (06630) 41233
⏰ Lunch and dinner

Paxoí (Paxos)
La Rosa di Paxos (€€)
Mihales Dahetos and his Italian wife run this delightful restaurant overlooking the harbour of Lákka. Choose from Greek and Italian dishes, and freshly caught fish cooked with herbs. Good choice of wines including a strong white from the family vineyard in Antipaxos. Reservations are advisable in high season.
✉ Lákka ☎ (06620) 31470
⏰ Lunch and dinner

Pélekas
Jimmy's (€€)
Jimmy and his family have been serving traditional Corfiot food here for over 25 years. It's a cheerful place and there are nicely furnished rooms with fine views if you want to stay.
✉ Pélekas village ☎ (06610) 94284 ⏰ Lunch and dinner

Levant Hotel Restaurant (€€)
High living at a high level. Eat on the terrace of this stylish hotel while the sun sets. Mediterranean cuisine to suit all tastes.
✉ By Kaiser's Lookout
☎ (06610) 94230
⏰ Lunch and dinner

Viros
Stamatis (€)
Popular and very friendly taverna. Should not be missed. Superb Corfiot food, *mezes* are a feast in themselves. Great house wine and impromptu music. It can get very busy so booking is advised.
✉ Viros (near Vríoni)
☎ (06610) 39249
⏰ Dinner. Closed Sun

Le Grand Balcon (€–€€)
Despite the name, this place serves up all Greek food from a huge menu. Situated in a remarkable position with views across Ipsos Bay. Reached from the Spartýlas road, or from the main coast road through a little gate, then up steep steps.
✉ On first hairpin bend of Spartýlas road above coast road junction ☎ (06610) 93958
⏰ Dinner

Fast Food
Fast food in Greece is fast becoming internationalised. *Tost* (toasted sandwiches with savoury fillings) are very popular, as are pizzas and hamburgers. But try *tiropita* (cheese pie, sometimes with egg), and *spanakopita* (spinach pie). When prepared well they are delicious, and addictive. *Gyros*, are Greek versions of fast-food shops, where large rounds of meat are grilled on revolving 'gyros'. The result is tasty kebabs and garnish, in pita bread.

97

Corfu Town

Prices

Approximate price for a double room for one night. (Prices are for the room, not per person.)

€	= under €35
€€	= €35–€65
€€€	= over €65

Checking In and Out

Hotel reception will ask for your passport on registering. It should be returned to you immediately the details have been recorded. Most hotels in the upper grades accept payment by credit card. Smaller, lower-grade hotels usually prefer cash. In Corfu Town there are a number of 24-hour cashpoints from which money can be withdrawn.

Arcadion (€€)

A 1960s building with a Venetian façade; fine position overlooking the end of the Liston and across the Esplanade to the Old Fortress. Great view from the front balconies, but street noise at night.

✉ 44 Kapodistrias ☎ (06610) 37671/37672; email: arcadion @otenet.gr ⏲ All year

Astron (€€)

Slightly cavernous and dated, but good value and handy for the Old Port, Esplanade and town centre. Overlooks Corfu Channel and Vidos.

✉ 15 Donzelot ☎ (06610) 39505/39986; fax (06610) 33708 ⏲ All year

Atlantis (€€)

Modern hotel at New Port, overlooking busy Xenofondos Stratigou Street. Several minutes' walk to town centre. Comfortable, well-appointed rooms. Very good restaurant and bar with impeccable service.

✉ 48 Xenofondos Stratigou ☎ (06610) 35560; email: atlanker@mail.otenet.gr ⏲ All year

Bella Venezia (€€–€€€)

Stylish hotel in refurbished classical mansion occupying the site of the original Bella Venezia destroyed in World War II. Charming gardens and a pavilion breakfast room and restaurant. In a quiet street close to centre.

✉ 4 N Zambeli ☎ (06610) 44290/46500; fax (06610) 20708 ⏲ Open all year

Bretagne (€€)

Well-appointed modern hotel on the southern outskirts of Corfu Town. Very close to the airport and consequently suffers some noise.

✉ 27 Georgaki Ethnicou Stadiou, Garitsa ☎ (06610) 30724/35690; fax (06610) 28027 ⏲ All year

Cavalieri (€€€)

In a beautifully reconstructed Venetian building at the quiet end of the Esplanade. The rooftop bar, open to non-residents, is an experience in itself, with marvellous evening ambience.

✉ 4 Kapodistrias ☎ (06610) 39041/39336; fax (06610) 39283; www.cavalieri-hotel.com ⏲ All year

Corfu Palace (€€€)

Top luxury hotel on seafront overlooking Garitsa Bay. Beautiful gardens, sun terraces, outdoor and indoor pools and a children's pool. *Haute cuisine* restaurant and in-house entertainment.

✉ 2 Leoforos Dimokratias ☎ (06610) 39485/39487; fax (06610) 31749; www.corfu palace.com ⏲ Apr–Oct

Hermes (€)

A budget hotel. The central position overlooking the bustling morning market is either a plus (atmosphere) or a minus (noisy), depending on your point of view.

✉ 14 G Markora Street ☎ (06610) 39321; fax (06610) 31747 ⏲ All year

Ionian (€)

Unglamourous but comfortable budget hotel. Handy for ferries, and ten minutes' walk from town centre and Esplanade. Front rooms can be noisy.

✉ 46 Xenefondos Stratigou ☎ (06610) 39915/30628; fax (06610) 44690 ⏲ All year

Around the Island

Acharávi

Acharávi Beach Hotel (€€)
Small, beach-side hotel with its own swimming pool, tennis, sports and restaurant.
✉ **Overlooking beach** ☎ (06630) 63102/63124; fax (06630) 63461; email: ach.b.ht @otenet.gr; 🕓 May–Oct

Ionian Princess (€€)
Sizeable, modern hotel a few minutes from the beach and with gardens, swimming pool, children's pool and playground, tennis, restaurant and in-house entertainment.
✉ **Between main road and beach** ☎ (06630) 63135; fax (06630) 63111; www.ionian princess.gr 🕓 May–Oct

Ágios Geórgios (Southwest)

Golden Sands Hotel (€–€€)
At the centre of the long straggling resort looking towards the sea. Handsome little church opposite in big open area adds a sense of spaciousness. The hotel has a swimming pool, children's play area, restaurant and bar.
✉ **Centre of resort** ☎ (06620) 51225; fax (06620) 51140 🕓 Apr–Oct

Ágios Górdis

Ayios Gordios Hotel (€–€€)
Set below spectacular coastal mountains in own gardens and with beach access. Swimming pool, tennis court, games.
✉ **Overlooking beach** ☎ (06610) 53320/53322; fax (06610) 52234; email: rizoresorts @sympria.com 🕓 Apr–Oct

Ákrotírio Komméno (Cape Komméno)

Grecotel Corfu Imperial (€€€)
Luxury-class hotel on peninsula, with sea views and set amid landscaped gardens. Large swimming pool, tennis courts, boutiques, beauty salon, restaurants, bars and access to private beaches.
✉ **Komméno–Gouviá** ☎ (06610) 91881; www.grecotel.gr 🕓 Apr–Oct

Alykés

Louis Kerkyra Golf (€€€)
Large, revamped, modern hotel offering numerous facilities including swimming pools, watersports, tennis, beach area, restaurants, bars and nightclub for *bouzouki*.
✉ **On main road 3km north of Corfu Town centre** ☎ (06610) 24030; fax (06610) 24080; www.louishotels.com 🕓 Apr–Oct

Aríllas

Aríllas Beach (€)
Small family-run hotel on seafront with basic, but comfortable accommodation. Popular restaurant.
✉ **On sea front** ☎ (06630) 51201; email: aktiarel@otenet.gr 🕓 Apr–Oct

Benítses

Potomaki (€)
Large hotel at heart of resort near beach. Own restaurant and swimming pool.
✉ **Near beach** ☎ (06610) 71140; fax (06610) 72451 🕓 Apr–Oct

Louis Regency (€€€)
Big hotel south of Benítses. Extensive sports facilities and access to beach below road. Beach-side taverna as well as restaurant.
✉ **South of Benitses** ☎ (06610) 71211/8; fax (06610) 71219; www.louishotels.com 🕓 Apr–Oct

Security and Safety

Greek people are noted for their honesty. Reputable hotels are generally secure and most have a safe or secure area for small items of value.

Most hotel lifts in Greece do not have cabin doors and the passing shaft wall is unguarded. Children, especially, should take great care.

Classification

Hotel rooms are graded by the Tourist Police into categories from L for Luxury, then from A to E in descending order of perceived quality. These classifications are based on facilities, not on position or character. All hotel rooms in Greece are required by law to display the room rates on a card, which is usually pinned to the inside of the room door. There are considerable seasonal variations in room rates. It is acceptable to negotiate a discount in the low season, especially if you plan to stay for more than two nights.

San Stefano (€€–€€€)

Modern hotel and apartments in a good position above resort. Large swimming pool, tennis courts, children's playground, restaurants, bars and shops. Courtesy bus to and from Benítses beach.

✉ **Above Benítses** ☎ (06610) 71112/8; fax (06610) 72272; email: sanstefano@hol.gr 🕐 Apr–Oct

Dasiá (Dassiá)
Amalia (€–€€)

On the main road and within easy reach of the beach, but manages to be fairly quiet. The hotel has its own swimming pool, restaurant and garden.

✉ **Dassiá–Káto Korakíana** ☎ (06610) 93523; fax (06610) 93720 🕐 Apr–Oct

Corfu Chandris Hotel/ Dassiá Chandris Hotel (€€–€€€)

Two luxury hotels adjacent to each other and under the same management. All modern amenities and direct access to beach. Swimming pools, children's play area, tennis courts, all watersports. Restaurants, bars, shops, in-house entertainment. Courtesy bus to and from Corfu Town.

✉ **Dassiá–Káto Korakíana** ☎ **Corfu Chandris/Dassiá Chandris** (06610) 97100/4;fax (06610) 93458; www.chandris.gr 🕐 Apr–Oct

Elea Beach (€€–€€€)

Large, modern hotel with own beachfront and gardens. All amenities, including nearby watersports centre.

✉ **Dassiá–Káto Korakíana** ☎ (06610) 93490/3; fax (06610) 93494; www.eleabeach.com 🕐 Apr–Oct

Paloma Bianca (€€)

Pleasant hotel in quiet location several minutes from beach and resort centre. Swimming pool and sports amenities, including tennis.

✉ **Dassiá–Káto Korakíana** ☎ (06610) 93575/6; fax (06610) 93577; email: palomole @otenet.gr 🕐 Apr–Oct

Érmones
Calimera Érmones Beach (€€–€€€)

Bungalow-style accommodation on terraced hillside with stairway or funicular ride to beach. Indoor and outdoor pools, gym, tennis courts and all types of watersports. In-house entertainment, restaurant, bars. The hotel operates a courtesy bus.

✉ **Overlooks beach** ☎ (06610) 94241/94243; fax (06610) 94248; www.sunmarotel ermones.gr 🕐 Apr–Oct

Glyfáda
Glyfáda Beach (€€)

Small, family-run hotel with basic but good facilities and not far from the beach.

✉ **North end of resort** ☎ and fax (06610) 94257/8 🕐 Apr–Oct

Louis Grand Hotel (€€–€€€)

Very large and luxurious hotel at far end of beach. Gardens and beach access. Many amenities, including tennis and a range of watersports. Restaurants, bars, shops.

✉ **South end of beach** ☎ (06610) 94140/5; www.louishotels.com 🕐 Apr–Oct

Gouviá
Aspa (€)

Small hotel with good basic amenities.

✉ **Near beach** ☎ (06610) 91165/91303 🕐 May–Oct

Louis Corcyra (€€€)
Smart luxury hotel with fine gardens and beach access. Numerous amenities, including tennis, squash, volleyball, games and a swimming pool.

✉ **Beachside location**
☎ **(06610) 90196/90198; fax (06610) 91591; www.louis hotels.com** 🕐 **Apr–Oct**

Park (€–€€)
Large, modern hotel in secluded wooded area. Good amenities include a swimming pool, tennis and volleyball. Ten minutes' walk to beach.

✉ **Outskirts of resort**
☎ **(06610) 91347/91310; fax (06610) 91531** 🕐 **Apr–Oct**

Ýpsos (Ipsos)
Ýpsos Beach (€€)
Off main road, but within a few minutes of the beach. Swimming pool, restaurant and in-house entertainment.

✉ **Outskirts of resort**
☎ **(06610) 93232; fax (06610) 93147** 🕐 **Apr–Oct**

Kanóni
Corfu Divani Palace (€€€)
Modern luxury hotel with gardens, sun terrace and swimming pool.

✉ **20 Nafsikas**
☎ **(06610) 38996/8; www.divanis.gr** 🕐 **Apr–Oct**

Corfu Holiday Palace (€€€)
Top-end luxury hotel complete with in-house casino (open to non-residents; strict dress code). Set in gardens with beach access and watersports. All amenities; indoor and outdoor pools, ten-pin bowling, gym and health club. Courtesy bus to and from Corfu Town

✉ **2 Nafsikas** ☎ **(06610) 36540; www.corfupalace.com**
🕐 **All year**

Kávos
Morfeas (€)
Close to beach but outside centre of resort. Facilities include swimming pool, rooftop restaurant, and there's in-house entertainment.

✉ **Near beach**
☎ **(06620) 61300/2**
🕐 **May–Oct**

San Marina (€€)
Alongside narrow beach but some distance from centre of resort. Swimming pool and watersports and other activities organised.

✉ **South end of resort**
☎ **(06620) 61345/6** 🕐 **May–Oct**

Kontókali (Kondókali)
Kontókali Bay (€€–€€€)
Luxury-class hotel in own gardens, with additional bungalow accommodation. Amenities include entertainment and watersports, children's club, tennis courts and swimming pools.

✉ **On peninsula by beaches**
☎ **(06610) 99000/2; fax (06610) 91901; www.kontokalibay.com**
🕐 **Apr–Oct**

Mesongí (Messongí)
Apollon Palace (€€)
Quality hotel with many facilities, including swimming pool, tennis, basketball and volleyball. Restaurant and bar.

✉ **Behind resort**
☎ **(06610) 75433/75035; fax (06610) 75602** 🕐 **Apr–Oct**

Christina (€€)
Attractive beach-side hotel with restaurant and well-equipped guest rooms. Few other amenities, but good service and position compensate.

✉ **Beachside location**
☎ **(06610) 76771**
🕐 **May–Oct**

Breakfast
The price of breakfast may or may not be included in the price of a room. Check details on registration. Hotel breakfasts can vary from rather dry affairs of croissants, rolls, bread, cake and jam, to a tasty selection of fruit juice, yoghurt, peaches, cereal, cold ham, cheese and boiled eggs. Coffee or tea is always served. Cooked breakfasts are available at some cafés and snack bars in many resorts.

Camping

Unofficial camping is illegal in Greece. There are a number of official campsites on Corfu, although, in the way of things, they may come and go. There are reputable campsites at the following resorts:

Corfu Camping
✉ Ýpsos (Ipsos)
☎ (06610) 93246
🕐 Seasonal

Dionysus Camping Village
✉ Dafnila/Dassiá
☎ (06610) 91760
🕐 Seasonal

Paleokastritsa Camping
✉ Paleokastritsa
☎ (06630) 41204
🕐 Seasonal

Moraïtika
Albatros (€–€€)

Close to beach and a few minutes from main street. Swimming pool and children's pool in surrounding gardens.
✉ Between main street and beach ☎ (06610) 75315/75317; fax (06610) 75484 🕐 Apr–Oct

Messongi Beach (€€)

Huge hotel dominating south end of beach, catering for guests' every need. Amenities include swimming pools, children's pool, tennis courts, sun terraces, children's play areas, plus restaurants, bars, beach-side taverna and café. The beach area is dense with thatched awnings. There are watersports and other events.
✉ South end of beach ☎ (06610) 76684; fax (06610) 75334; email: aktimes @otenet.gr 🕐 Apr–Oct

Miramare Beach (€€–€€€)

Luxury hotel in own grounds fronted by narrow beach. Gardens lead down to beach-side bar. Tennis courts. Courtesy bus service to Corfu Town.
✉ Near centre of beach ☎ (06610) 75224/75226; fax (06610) 75305; www.miramare beach.gr 🕐 May–Oct

Nisáki (Nissaki)
Nissaki Beach Hotel (€€–€€€)

A luxury hotel in a prime coastal position. Facilities include a swimming pool, tennis courts; even crazy golf. Exclusive beach area below has all watersports and amenities, including beach-side taverna.
✉ In own grounds ☎ (06630) 91232/91233; fax (06630) 22079; email: nissaki@otenet.gr 🕐 Apr–Oct

Palaiokastrítsa (Paleokastritsa)
Akrotiri Beach (€€–€€€)

In a spectacular setting on the neck of a wooded peninsula directly above the beach. All the usual amenities, including a swimming pool.
✉ Overlooks main bay ☎ (06630) 41237; fax (06630) 41277; email: belunht@hol.gr 🕐 Apr–Oct

Hotel Oceanis (€€)

In a stunning position on rocky promontory overlooking the bay, with a sun terrace and swimming pool. Access to pebble beach. Restaurant and in-house entertainment.
✉ Centre of resort ☎ (06630) 41230; fax (06630) 22368; email: oceanis@hol.gr 🕐 Apr–Oct

Zephyros (€)

Basic but comfortable amenities and near beach. Pets allowed.
✉ Near centre of resort ☎ and fax (06630) 41244 🕐 Apr–Oct

Paxoí (Paxos)
Paxos Club (€€€)

Luxury hotel with some apartments as well. Big swimming pool, restaurant and bar. In-house entertainment.
✉ About 2km outside Gáios ☎ (06620) 32450 🕐 May–Sep

Pélekas
Levant (€€–€€€)

Peaceful, elegant hotel in enviable setting on hill top, near famous Kaiser's

Lookout. Friendly, family-run and decorated with antiques. Facilities include restaurant, swimming pool and terrace from which to enjoy the sunset extravaganza.

✉ **Above Pélekas village** ☎ **(06610) 94230; fax (06610) 94115; www.levanthotel.com** 🕓 **All year**

Tzovana (€)
Small hotel without too many frills. There is a swimming pool and organised activities.

✉ **About 1.5km from beaches** ☎ **(06610) 94594; fax (06610) 94738** 🕓 **Apr–Oct**

Pérama
Aelos Beach (€€)
Very large hotel on hillside above Pérama. Several minutes to beach and to resort itself. Numerous in-house amenities include swimming pool, sun terrace and pool-side bar. Children's play area. Watersports organised at beach. Pets allowed.

✉ **Overlooks resort** ☎ **(06610) 33132/6; fax (06610) 40420** 🕓 **Apr–Oct**

Alexandros (€€–€€€)
Situated at heart of resort a few minutes from shingle beach. There is a swimming pool in quiet gardens with attendant taverna. Watersports and other activities organised.

✉ **Mid resort** ☎ **(06610) 36855/6; fax (06610) 33160** 🕓 **Mar–Oct**

Pérama (€)
A small hotel on main road through resort. Basic amenities. Handy for beach.

✉ **Pérama** ☎ **(06610) 33167; fax (06610) 40880** 🕓 **Apr–Oct**

Róda
Róda Beach (€€)
Very large hotel with additional bungalow accommodation. Swimming pools, children's pool area, sun terrace, tennis court. Set in large gardens with access to the beach.

✉ **Beachside near west end of resort** ☎ **(06630) 64181/5; fax (06630) 63436; email: rodabeach village@in.gr** 🕓 **Apr–Sep**

Silver Beach (€€)
This is a small hotel with good-quality facilities. Swimming pool, bar and gardens. A few minutes' walk to the beach.

✉ **In village** ☎ **(06630) 63112/63134; fax (06630) 63076** 🕓 **Apr–Sep**

Sidári
Afroditi Beach (€€)
Small beach-side hotel with main facilities and a swimming pool.

✉ **Overlooks beach** ☎ **and fax (06630) 95247** 🕓 **Apr–Sep**

Selas (€€)
Medium-sized hotel in a quiet location away from the centre of Sidári and a few minutes from a beach.

✉ **Outskirts of resort** ☎ **(06630) 95285** 🕓 **Apr–Sep**

Parking
Local people are experts at casual parking but you are not advised to copy them. Corfu Town has convenient official parking areas in Old Port Square and on the Spianáda (Esplanade). Parking areas usually have an attendant who will issue a parking card. By the New Fortress there is a small parking area reached from Xenefondos Stratigou, by turning right up Lohagou Spyrou Vaikou Street alongside the west wall of the New Fortress.

Corfu Town

Bargaining

Greece takes the middle ground between the western culture of fixed-price shopping and oriental bargaining, or 'haggling'. Greeks love a good haggle and so should you. Although fixed-priced shopping is the norm, especially in Corfu Town, where brand name shops and speciality shops predominate, you may still get a flavour of bargaining at local markets. Try also the side-street shops bedecked with clothes, rugs and general goods and the roadside stalls of places such as Makrádes (▶ 77) on the northwest coast. It is only really acceptable to haggle over non-perishable goods.

The majority of resorts on Corfu have a supermarket plus a sprinkling of gold and silver jewellers, summer clothes' boutiques, leather-goods' shops and gift shops. However, most close down for the winter.

Corfu Town is the main all-year-round shopping centre of the island. It has all the general outlets you would expect to find in a comparable urban centre, from hardware shops to food and drink suppliers, from fashion and clothes shops to the *periptero* kiosks which sell everything from newspapers and cigarettes, to sweets and soft drinks, soap and condoms. There are some excellent wine and spirit stores and many mouth-watering *zaharoplastios*, shops that specialise in cakes, pastries and sweets. Specialities to look out for in Corfu include perishables, such as olives, herbs, spices, nuts, and cheeses such as the soft white feta, made from goat and sheep milk. Virgin olive oil can be bought in supermarkets as well as in delicatessens. A drink special to the island is Kumquat (see panel ▶ 107).

Gold and silver shops have proliferated in Corfu in recent years and offer quite good bargains compared with mainstream European outlets. There are numerous shops selling jewellery, leather goods and ceramics in Corfu Town, and similar shops can be found in most resorts. Reproduction icons and religious objects are on sale at a number of outlets. They range in price from a few thousand drachmas to tens of thousands of drachmas.

Books, Newspapers and Magazines

Kiosk

A newspaper and magazine shop behind the Liston with an astonishing international selection from fashion magazines to hobbies.

✉ **11 Kapodistrias (behind the Liston). Also at Old Port**
☎ **(06610) 42760**

Lycoudis

Wide range of books; mainly Greek publications, but with a good selection of guide books. Some local books translated into English, German, Italian and French. Paperback novels in English.

✉ **65 E Voulgareos**
☎ **(06610) 39845**

Clothing

Backcover

Quality casual wear and swimwear. Top brand names include French Connection, Calvin Klein and Henri Lloyd.

✉ **51/53 N Theotoki**

The Beauty Shop

Cosmetics and perfumes by names such as Revlon and Estée Lauder. Also Marks and Spencer underwear.

✉ **G Theotoki and Alexandras Avenue**

Body Shop

Same range as carried by Body Shop internationally. English-speaking staff.

✉ **St Spyridon's Square (Plateía Iroon Kypriakou Agonos)**

English Imports

Range of clothing and household goods, some non-perishable food items, English newspapers and books. Friendly staff.

✉ **1st Parados Mitropoliti Methodiou** (on corner with San Rocco Square, signposted down alleyway) ☎ **(06610) 47692**

Famous Names
Imported chain store goods to suit all the family.
✉ **50 I Theotoki Street**
☎ **(06610) 49313**

Harley Boutique/Smash Kerkira Ltd
Trendy leather clothes and accessories.
✉ **12B Eth Antistasseos, New Port** ☎ **(06610) 36600/44064**

The Levi's Shop
Famous-name supplier of everything from jeans to belts and hats.
✉ **Corner of San Rocco Square and Mitropoliti Methodiou Street**

Lido Vois Moda
For dedicated shoppers. This multi-store experience has five floors of fashions for men and women. Mainly quality Italian imports. Clothes and accessories, from shoes to evening wear.
✉ **100 Evgeniou Voulgareos Street**

The London Shop
Lots of imported goods, including underwear, jewellery and fashion accessories.
✉ **18 Pol Konstanta Street (in shopping arcade)**
☎ **(06610) 24791**

Praxis
Always popular with the young. Levi jeans and casual wear by O'Neill and Diesel.
✉ **N Theotoki**

Simon's T-shirts
Promotional T-shirts and screen printing.
✉ **20 Spiridonas Gardikiot (signposted down sidestreet)**
☎ **(06610) 33025**

Crafts, Antiques, Jewellery and Ceramics

Aypa Ceramics
Selection of ceramic ware and other artefacts.
✉ **28 Paleologou**
☎ **(06610) 49100**

CFJ
Handmade jewellery in classical Greek, Byzantine or modern styles, located in the old Venetian town.
✉ **Filellinon 16**
☎ **(06610) 39054**

Costa Marollas
Jewellery designs in gold, silver and other materials.
✉ **E Voulgareos**

Esplanada Jewellers
Large selection of gold and silverware, and other items.
✉ **Vas Georgiou 20**
☎ **(06610) 45796**

Fos tis Anatolis
Stylish Greek crafts: silverware, rugs, glass, jewellery and ceramics.
✉ **8 Kapodistriou**

Libra
Gold, silverware, jewellery.
✉ **1 Vrachlioti Square**
☎ **(06610) 44924**

Mercury Design
Hand-crafted Greek jewellery in gold and silver.
✉ **16 Alipio** ☎ **(06610) 21631**

Ministry of Culture Museum Shop
Just inside the entrance archway to the Old Fortress, this bookshop and gallery sells seriously expensive art and archaeological replicas.
✉ **Old Fortress**
☎ **(06610) 46919**

Mohamed Koriem Ceramics
Attractive ceramic ware and other craftwork.
✉ **56 Guilford (Town Hall Square)** ☎ **(06610) 45610**

Public Toilets
There are very few public toilets in Corfu. Tavernas and restaurants must have toilets by law. The Greek for 'Gents' is *andron*, and for 'Ladies' is *gynaikon*. Public toilets may not have toilet paper available.

Public toilets in Corfu Town
✉ **Kapodistrias Street (on southern half of the Esplanade). Facility for disabled**
✉ **San Rocco Square. At west end, down steps. Not always at their best. Brace yourself...**

In Greece, the circumference of waste pipes is small and outlets are easily blocked by toilet paper. However fastidious you may be, you should comply with local custom and dispose of toilet paper in the receptacles supplied in accommodation, restaurants, tavernas and bars, entertainment premises, and public toilets.

Newspapers and Magazines

Most daily newspapers from Britain and Northern Europe are on sale in Corfu the day after publication. Weekly digests of some dailies are also available. Magazines of all types are on sale in the famous Kiosk (▶ 104) and in newsagents and *peripteros* (kiosks). An excellent English-language newspaper is *The Corfiot*, published monthly. It contains news and features on island life and some very useful listings and advertisements. The multi-language *Terra Kerkyra* is a local magazine, up-dated each year, containing a great deal of information and with excellent listings of restaurants, tavernas and entertainments.

'Adult' Souvenirs

In Greece, many tourist-oriented shops do not distinguish between 'adult' souvenirs and those suitable for anyone: you are quite likely to find pornographic books, playing cards, videos etc stacked right next to children's toys or the cash till, rather than discreetly out of sight or on a top shelf. This is something to bear in mind when shopping with children in tow.

Olive Wood Workshop

Carved wooden objects, both decorative and functional. Imaginative designs, large and small.

✉ 27 Filarmonikis 54 G Theotoki ☎ (06610) 40621

Terracotta

In the heart of the Campiello, the old part of Corfu Town, this stylish shop has a good selection of jewellery, ceramics and sculptures and specialises in contemporary Greek art and crafts.

✉ 2 Filarmonikis
☎ (06610) 45260

Theofanis Sp. Lykissas

Replica icons, candles and ecclesiastical objects.

✉ 18 St Spyridon's Square (Plateía Iroon Kypriakou Agonos)
☎ (06610) 47397

Food and Drink

Andriotis

Traditional confectionery such as *mandoláto* (almond nougat), *mandoles* (burnt sugared almonds), walnut chocolate, as well as bottles of Kumquat in the shape of Corfu.

✉ Arlioti Maniarizi 1
☎ (06610) 38045

Costas Thimis

Terrific selection of wines, spirits and liqueurs.

✉ N Theotoki

Kriticos

Irresistible selection of sweets to ruin any holiday diet you might forlornly be considering. Charming service.

✉ Town Hall Square
☎ (06610) 40444 ✉ G Theotoki
☎ (06610) 26676

Marcos Margossian

This wonderful coffee, wine and spirit shop also sells sweets and biscuits. Courteous service.

✉ 20 G Theotoki Avenue, (south side, opposite Pallas Cinema)

Nostos

Tasty cakes, pastries and desserts. Wines and spirits.

✉ St Spyridon's Square (Plateía Iroon Kypriakou Agonos). On approach to Church of St Spyridon ☎ (06610) 47714

Starenio

Traditional bread, honey cake, and sweet biscuits of numerous delicious flavours.

✉ Guilford ☎ (06610) 47370

Market and Main Shopping Areas

Fruit and Vegetable Market

Corfu Town's lively morning market beneath the walls of the New Fortress, has an excellent selection of fruit, vegetables and all types of edible olives. Fresh fish is also sold and there are a few peripheral sellers of clothes and souvenirs.

✉ G Markora
🕐 Mon–Sat 7–1:30

G Theotoki/Voulgareos

A range of shops of all types.

✉ Main linking streets that run northeast from San Rocco Square to the Old Town

Mitropoliti Methodiou

Middle-market clothes, shoe and hardware shops.

✉ Street running southwest from San Rocco Square

N Theotoki

Numerous fashion shops, jewellers, wines and spirits.

✉ Runs from behind the Liston towards the New Fortress

Sevastianou Street

Great selection of stylish fashion and shoe shops.

✉ Runs from behind the Liston to M Theotoki Street

Xenofondos Stratigou

Ships' chandlers, engineering shops and hardware shops.

✉ Main road running west between the Old Port and the New Port

Around the Island

Apart from food stores, most shops in resorts close down during the winter months (November to March).

Acharávi
Dala's Gold
A very smart gold- and silver-jewellery shop with various designer wear.
✉ **Main street, near west end of resort**

Elea
'Elea' in Greek means olive tree, and everything here, including the shop itself, is made of olive wood.
✉ **Main street, in centre**

Gastoúri
Distillery Vassilakis
Unmissable. You will be 'spirited' inside before you are half in or out of the Achilleion gates opposite. Vassilakis has a huge selection of wines, spirits and liqueurs, as well as numerous Kumquat products.
✉ **Opposite the Achilleion**
☎ **(06610) 52440**

Ýpsos (Ipsos)
T-Shirt Market
Every T-shirt and motif you might have forgotten to bring is available here.
✉ **Main street**

Kassiópi
Agatha's Lace
A centre of Corfu lace-making, with a good selection of handmade lace goods and rugs on offer.
✉ **Main Street**
☎ **(06630) 81315**

Kontókali (Kondókali)
The Beer Bucket
The Beer Bucket offers a large range of imported British food and drink.
✉ **Inner Road**
☎ **(06610) 90750**

Makrádes
The village of Makrádes (▶ 77) on the northwest coast of Corfu has become famous for its roadside stalls selling souvenirs, embroidered table linen, knitwear, ceramics, carpets, lace and a range of other goods. A great deal of noisy touting and brash sales talk goes on. The experience is part of the deal.
✉ **Main road, 35km northwest of Corfu Town**

Paxos
The Mulberry Tree
Local produce including homemade wine and olive oil. English-run.
✉ **In the village of Vístonas**
☎ **(06630) 49049**
🕐 **Daily in season 9:30–5:30**

Other Outlets

Ameco Distillery
An exhibition combined with a tastery.
✉ **Eth Paleokastritsa (13km from Corfu Town)**
☎ **(06630) 49083**

Stinis Cellar
This is the place to find out about wine making on Corfu amid huge stocks of the stuff. There is a storage cellar and a wine 'talking shop'. Countless varieties of wine, bottled and from the barrel are available. Also ouzo and *tsipouro*.
✉ **42 Eth Paleokastritsa**
☎ **(06610) 46705**

Kumquat
This is a famous Corfiot liqueur. It is distilled from the tiny kumquat, a citrus fruit that looks like a miniature orange. It is native to South East Asia and was introduced to Corfu in the 1860s. The standard Kumquat drink is bright orange, the colour being derived from the rind; it is very sweet. There is a colourless distillation of Kumquat juice which is far more potent and adventurous and can be identified by the 'twig' with attached crystals that floats inside the bottle. All manner of other drinks, candies, and sweets are produced using kumquats.

Children's Attractions

Corfiot Children

Corfiot children are very adept at entertaining themselves. Swimming is often second nature to local youngsters and basketball and football are both Greek obsessions. In Corfu, as in all of Greece, children are well-integrated into adult society. Yours will be welcomed in tavernas where local people are happy for them to be seen and heard – within reason...

Beach Law

All beaches in Greece are freely accessible to the public by law. On Corfu, as elsewhere, many beach front hotels monopolise the area of beach in front of their premises. The law states that free passage along the shore must not be blocked with any permanent structure. If you simply wish to lie on a beach for a short while, you are free to do so. You are not bound to rent any moveable equipment that is set out on that beach, although you should not use such equipment without first paying for its use.

Safe Beaches

Most of Corfu's beaches have safe bathing, with shallow water extending for some distance over sand and shingle and with an absence of currents. Where steep shelving occurs on beaches, or where there may be potentially dangerous currents, this is mentioned in the text.

Tidal movements in the Mediterranean generally are minimal, although there may be some visible change in the waterline especially on the west coast beaches. At some beaches, more sand builds up, or is exposed, in summer.

East Coast

Beaches on Corfu's east coast are mainly shingle and often quite narrow. They are usually very safe for bathing and are easily accessible from the main coast road. All types of beach equipment and watersports are available at most coastal resorts. Because of these advantages, the beaches can become very crowded.

Best beaches for children include:
Ágios Stéfanos (Northwest) (➤ 55), Barmbáti (➤ 61), Dassiá (➤ 65), Gouviá (➤ 69), Kalámi (➤ 20), Messongí (➤ 77) and Moraïtika (➤ 78).

North Coast

Corfu's north coast beaches are generally much longer than their east coast counterparts and have more sand. They tend to be narrow, but do not shelve steeply into the sea, thus making them safe for very small children. These beaches may be affected in the afternoons by onshore winds. Every type of beach equipment and watersport is available at most of these beaches.

Best beaches for children include:
Acharávi (➤ 49), Róda (➤ 86) and Sidári (➤ 88).

West Coast

Corfu's west coast beaches are much sandier than those on the east coast and they are often longer and wider. They are less accessible – many are reached down long, winding roads – and may be affected by wind at times. The prevailing wind in summer is known as the *maistro*; it blows from between northwest and west northwest. This makes for ideal windsurfing conditions at the two Ágios Geórgios beaches (➤ 50), and the beaches at Ágios Górdis (➤ 51) and Glyfáda (➤ 69). The *maistro* is variable in strength, but usually rises in the afternoon and drops away in the evening. A disadvantage of this breeziness, on the more open west coast beaches, is that sand may become windblown. Most types of beach equipment and watersport are available at the more accessible and popular resorts.

Best beaches for children include:
Ágios Geórgios (Northwest) (➤ 50), Ágios Górdis (➤ 51) and Glyfáda, beach shelves steeply in places, (➤ 69).

Cycling

General advice on cycling is covered in the Peace and Quiet section (▶ 12–13). Cycling on Corfu's public roads is not advised for very young children or for those who are inexperienced. There is, however, a vast network of off-road tracks which can be enjoyed. The best areas are in the low-lying southern part of Corfu and in the northern coastal strip behind Sidári, Róda and Acharávi. Children should not explore off-road tracks by bike on their own as they will almost certainly get lost. For bike-hire outlets ▶ 114.

Festivals

Local festivals (▶ 116) are excellent entertainment for children on holiday (adults too), not least because local youngsters take part wholeheartedly. There is always something going on, and even in the lulls, the Corfiots generate an atmosphere of excitement and goodwill.

Go-karts

Several resorts have go-kart circuits. The suitability of these is left to parental judgement.

There are go-kart circuits at:
Barmbáti
Dassiá
Kávos
Pyrgi
Sidári

Horse Riding

There are several riding stables on Corfu. Most cater for children and a family outing on horseback can be delightful. For riding stables ▶ 115.

Water Parks

Aqualand (€€€)

Corfu's water-fun park with a wide range of waterslides, swimming pools and other aquatic attractions.
✉ **Ágios Ionnas (on Pélekas–Érmones road)**
☎ **(06610) 58351/52963; www.aqualand.com.gr**
🚌 **Blue bus 8 from Plateia San Rocco, Corfu Town to Aqualand**
🕐 **Daily May–Jun, Sep–Oct 10–6, Jul–Aug 10–7**

Hydropolis (€€€)

Not a patch on Aqualand, but provides a diversion for families: waterslides, pools and pet corner. Also incorporates a sports centre with gym and tennis courts.
✉ **On main road, on Kassiopi side of Acharávi**
☎ **(06630) 64700**

Water Slides

There are small water slides at:
Ágios Geórgios (Northwest),
Moraïtika
Sidári

Watersports

Most of Corfu's popular beaches provide facilities for various watersports, ranging from waterskiing and paragliding, to pedaloes and canoes. Banana boats and ringos, which involve inflated floats being towed behind speedboats, appeal to children and young people. Banana boats are generally a safe option, but ringo-riding, in which you sit inside an inflated inner tube is a fairly robust experience and is not suited to young children. Some beaches, such as Moraïtika (▶ 78), have ringo-riding for children.

Water Safety

Some beaches in Corfu have a system of safety signals that indicate whether or not prevailing conditions are safe for watersports or swimming. Signals may vary. If any signal, usually a coloured flag, is displayed, its significance should be checked and its instruction heeded.

General Safety

Guard against sunburn and sunstroke. A holiday can be ruined in the first few days from too much exposure to the sun. Take precautions by using reputable sun-screening creams and by rationing your sunbathing. Be very careful not to expose young children to the sun for long periods. There are not many sea hazards on Ionian beaches, but keep an eye out for jellyfish, and for sea urchins near rocks.

Miscellaneous Attractions

There are numerous boat excursions from the larger resorts. Regular ferries ply between the Old Port and Vídos Island. *The Calypso Star*, a glass-bottomed boat, runs trips round the island from the Old Port. In Corfu Town, on the Esplanade, trips can be made in horse-drawn carriages.

Music and Nightlife

Staying Legal

It is neither polite nor wise to make discourteous public comments about the Greek religion, culture or the State. Such action may be judged as an offence and treated as such by the police.

Recreational drug use, and especially supplying drugs of any kind, is considered a major crime. Supplying even small amounts of drugs may result in a very long sentence of up to life imprisonment. In the event of arrest for any matter, you have the right to contact your consulate.

Corfu Town

Bars

Cavalieri Hotel Roof Garden
The candlelit roof terrace overlooking the town and bay provides the perfect spot for an evening cocktail or light meal.

✉ **4 Kapodistriou Street**
☎ **(06610) 39041**
🕐 **In season 6:30PM–1AM**

Dirty Dick's
There is a good atmosphere in this unsophisticated venue on Old Port Square. Price of drinks is below average.

✉ **Old Port Square, Spilia**
🕐 **All day**

Dogma
An ideal place for those with quieter tastes, with a medieval ambience and good service. Price of drinks is average.

✉ **Mandouki Square, New Port** ☎ **(06610) 24545**
🕐 **10PM–3:30AM**

Don Juan (€–€€)
A café-bar in the old Mandouki area behind New Port, situated in a restored building with archways and a paved floor. There is a garden area. Classical, modern and Greek music. Selection of coffees, wines, spirits and beers.

✉ **57 Xenofontos Stratigou Street, Mandouki** 🕐 **All day**

Mermaid
Nicely placed bar in a narrow street between Kapodistrias and M Theotoki Street with a 'city' feel to it. The Mermaid is popular with British residents and long-term Corfu devotees. Price of drinks is average.

✉ **Ágios Pandon Street, off the Liston**

Mobile
Greek music at a friendly venue. Price of drinks is above average.

✉ **52 Eth Antistasseos Street**
🕐 **From midday onwards**

Cinemas

Greek cinemas show all the mainstream American and European films and English-language films, are subtitled in Greek. The sound quality is usually good. There is a frustrating, though amusing tendency to interrupt films at reel breaks, often at critical moments of tension, so that everyone can rush to the foyer for snacks and frantic smoking. This can produce a level of barely contained excitement that is an entertainment in itself.

Orfeus
Smaller venue with good selection of films, usually in English with Greek subtitles.

✉ **Corner of Akadimias Street and Aspioti Street**
☎ **(06610) 39768**

Phoenix
Open-air, summer-only cinema showing Greek and foreign films.

✉ **1 Ioánnou G. Daliétou**
☎ **(06610) 37428** 🕐 **Jun–Aug**

Concerts

Old Fortress
Open-air sound and light extravaganzas in the Old Fortress during the summer. Performances are in English, Greek, French and Italian. There are also

performances of traditional folk dance.

✉ **Old Fortress, Esplanade**
☎ (06610) 48310/48311
🕐 **Evening performance**

The Esplanade

During the summer months there are musical performances at the bandstand on the Esplanade.

Theatre

Municipal Theatre of Corfu

Fairly regular performances by groups such as Corfu's Municipal Choir. Musical events, opera, drama and dance. There is a licensed bar.

✉ **G Theotoki**
☎ (06610) 37520

Dance Clubs and Discos

Corfu has many dance clubs and music bars, all of which play contemporary styles of music. The DJs in the bigger clubs are often British and they play the dance music currently popular in Northern Europe.

The dance clubs and music bars of Corfu Town are concentrated at the demurely named Entertainment Centre, better known as 'The Disco Strip', a few kilometres west of the New Port on Ethnikis Antistasseos, the main road from the town to the north and west. The road is very busy with traffic late into the night. In places it is without safe pedestrian walkways. When travelling to and from the clubs it is probably safer to do so by taxi or bus rather than on foot. The average price for a drink is about euro3. There is an admission charge at some clubs.

Coca Club

A long-established, comparatively sophisticated dance club with a garden cocktail bar and good music.

Go late to see it in full swing. Drinks are on the pricy side.

✉ **30 Eth Antistasseos Street**
☎ (06610) 34477
🕐 **From midnight onwards**

Ekati Music Hall

Best known for its *bouzouki* band, the Ekati is a stylish, expensive nightclub on the edge of Corfu Town. Large bar, dancing hall; dinners are available.

✉ **Alikes Potomós Street**
☎ (06610) 45920 🕐 **Daily midnight to late, winter Fri and Sat only**

Electron

Electron offers an interesting mix of Greek and European dance music in a tropical ambience. Price of drinks is above average.

✉ **Eth Antistasseos Street**
☎ (06610) 26793

Hippodrome

The club with the pool. Big venue catering for 2,000 clubbers, hopefully not all of them in the pool. There is a mix of connecting levels, both indoors and outdoors with exotic palms and bar-top dancers. Also Club Prive, a chill-out zone with Greek music, food, wine and coffee. The Hippodrome is open in the mornings for coffee, drinks, food and swimming. Price of drinks is above average. The entrance fee includes one drink.

✉ **52 Eth Antistasseos Street**
☎ (06610) 43150
🕐 **11PM onwards**

Sax

Late-night with live rock music and all-night dancing.

✉ **48 Eth Antistasseos Street**
☎ (06610) 21757
🕐 **Daily midnight to late**

Philharmonic Societies

There are 18 marching bands, or Philharmonic Societies, on Corfu. The Corfu Town bands include the oldest, founded in 1840 as the St Spyrídon Philharmonic. The band, whose members wear red uniforms, became known later as the 'Old' Philharmonic after the founding of another society in 1890, the Mantzaros Philharmonic or 'New' Philharmonic, which has a blue uniform. Another Philharmonic Society is the Kapodistrias Philharmonic Union, founded in 1980. The bands and their stirring classical music are an unforgettable part of Corfu's religious and cultural festivals.

Classical and Traditional

Corfu's strong musical tradition is also maintained by the Corfu Symphony Orchestra and Choir, while the students of the Music Department of the Ionian University often perform traditional Greek music in public. The bandstand at the south end of the Esplanade is often the venue for concerts by the Philharmonic Societies and other performers.

Gambling

The island's only casino, at the Corfu Holiday Palace, offers the usual facilities including roulette. It is open to non-residents. A strict dress code applies and a passport is required for entrance.

✉ **2 Nafsikas, Kanóni**
☎ **(06610) 36540**
🕐 **All year**

Driving Hazards

Driving on Corfu can sometimes be nerve-wracking for those used to well-ordered traffic systems. Signposting at busy junctions may be erratic and road works can sometimes appear unexpectedly. Country roads, never meant for anything other than farm and rural traffic, have deep potholes in places. If encountered at speed these can be devastating to tyres, wheels, suspensions and holiday budgets. Mountain roads may have poor cambers and unprotected roadside ditches. On the descent of steep hairpin bends, loose gravel can cause skidding unless speed is reduced to the minimum and braking is gradual. At junctions with busy roads and dual carriageways, remember that traffic is coming from your immediate left.

Around the Island

Dance Venues and Bars

Resorts such as Kávos, Benítses, Kassiópi and Ipsos are known for late-night dance club action. Most of the popular resorts have clubs and music bars. Bars often aim for the atmosphere of British pubs, many have satellite television and videos on big screens. Clubs may change hands from season to season.

Acharávi
The Sail Inn

Popular dance club in the main street. Looks like a wooden stockade from the outside. Inside there is a dance area, outside there is a large cocktail bar and floodlit palm trees. Admission is free after midnight.

✉ **Main road, by roundabout where road to Epískepsi turns off**

Benítses

A range of music bars and clubs, all offering much the same in music and a fairly frantic atmosphere. Includes Tribal Club Cafe, B-52s, The Rainbow Pub, G-Spot, Alcoholics Anonymous and Valentino's.

Dasiá (Dassiá)
Edem Cocktail Bar

Lasers and videos at this beach-side venue and all-night music and dancing. Price of drinks is average.

✉ **On Dassiá beach**
☎ **(06610) 93013**
🕐 **10:30AM–late**

Érmones
Morrison Café

Pleasant sunset venue with big outdoor area and tree-shaded garden. Mix of musical styles including contemporary, jazz and traditional folk music. Price of drinks is average.

✉ **Overlooking the beach at Érmones**
☎ **(06610) 94080**
🕐 **4PM onwards**

Glyfáda
Aloha Beach Club

All-day venue with dance music. Restaurant offering breakfast, lunch and *mezes* in the evening. Wine from the barrel. Price of drinks is above average.

✉ **By entrance to beach**
☎ **(06610) 94380**
🕐 **10AM until late**

Ýpsos (Ipsos)/Pyrgi

Still fairly devoted to late-night fun and games, typical venues include News, Bar 52, Hector's, the Temple Bar, Monaco Disco, the Albatross Club, Dirty Nellies, Paradise Bar and CJ's.

Kassiópi

Big choice of clubs and music bars including Eclipse, a leading venue, the Axis Club, Angelos and Jasmine.

Kávos

Future is the biggest venue. Its brassy, glittering façade is enough to make your head spin and DJs from Northern Europe ensure the music is up-to-date. Other lively clubs and bars include Empire Club ('Every Night a Saturday Night' is the promise); Paradise, The Face, The Venue, Bad Boyz Club, 42nd Street, Mr Bean Bar, Rolling Stone Music Bar, Xanadu Club, Whispers Disco and many more. Captain Kostas Bar for Greek dancing.

Moraïtika
Charlie's Bar

Popular and long-established bar with Charlie Chaplin motif.
✉ **Main street**

Paleokastritsa
The Paleo Club

A small venue at entrance to resort, approached by a stiff hike from sea level to get your legs in trim. Garden area

and contemporary dance music.

✉ **Paleokastritsa (by junction with road to Lákones)**
🕐 **Late evening until late**

Pélekas

Banana Club

Open-air dancing all night with DJs playing a selection of old and new dance music. Free entrance.

✉ **On the road to Glyfáda**

Pélekas Café

Venue with a view. Contemporary and occasional live Greek music.

✉ **In village** ☎ **(06610) 95104**
🕐 **Lunch and dinner**

Sidári

Discos and dance clubs include Remezzo and Caesar's (► 88). La Notte nightclub is just across the Loxida River. The Palazzo Bar, in the centre, has a good choice of cocktails and beers from the barrel. The Pipestrelo Pub has regular Greek evenings for a change.

Tzavros

Corfu By Night

An authentic *bouzouki* club, popular with locals. Greek music and ambience. Occasional Greek dancers. Drinks and (Greek) food are pricy. To see it at its best go after midnight at the weekend.

✉ **Eth Paleokastritsa Road beyond the turning to Ipsos**
☎ **(06610) 91733**

Museums, Art Galleries and Exhibitions

Archaeological Museum (► 23)

Art Café Gallery

Small gallery staging exhibitions by Corfiot and contemporary artists and craftspeople.

✉ **Palace of St Michael and St**

George, East Wing, Esplanade, Corfu Town
🕐 **11AM–2PM, 6–9PM**

Byzantine Museum (► 36)

Castello Art Gallery

Modern building in grounds of old mansion. Exhibition of works on loan from Greek National Art Gallery

✉ **Kato Korakiana**
🕐 **10AM–2PM, 6–9PM**

Faliraki Ionian Cultural Centre

In refurbished medieval building behind the Palace of St Michael and St George. Complex includes a gallery and the Church of St Nicholas.

✉ **Murayia, St Nicholas Gate, Corfu Town**

Folklore Museum of Central Corfu (► 90)

Kapodistrias Museum

Memorabilia of John Capodistrias, first president of a united Greece.

✉ **Koukoritsa, near Evropoúli village, 5km west of Corfu Town**
☎ **(06610) 39528**
🕐 **11AM–1PM Wed and Sat only**

Municipal Art Gallery (► 34)

Municipal Theatre of Corfu

Art exhibitions are held in the theatre foyer.

✉ **G Theotoki**
☎ **(06610) 33598**

Museum of Asiatic Art (► 40)

New Fortress Gallery (► 38)

Paper Money Museum (► 42)

Petsalis Art Gallery

✉ **3 Vrachlioti Street, Corfu Town** ☎ **(06610) 34296**

Solomos Museum (► 36)

Churches

The Greek Orthodox Church is the official Church on Corfu and is strongly represented, although with its history of Venetian and later British presence the island has always supported other denominations, too.

The Roman Catholic cathedral is located in the Town Hall Square (► 43). From 1 June to 30 September, Mass is celebrated Sunday at 8:30AM, 10AM and 7PM. From 1 October to 31 May, Mass is celebrated on Sundays at 8AM, 9AM, 10AM and 6PM.

Holy Trinity Anglican Church is located at the east end of the old Parliament building at 21 Mavili Street ☎ (06610) 31467.

Sunday morning prayers are at 9:45AM; Holy Communion at 10:30AM; Songs of Praise at 7PM on the first and third Sundays of each month.

The Evangelical Church of Greece is located at 3 Iakovou Polila Street ☎ (06610) 37304. Sunday morning service is held at 10:30AM; evening service at 7PM.

Sport, Water Sports & Outdoor Activities

Cricket

Corfu's unique cricketing tradition is a legacy of the British Protectorate. For nearly 50 years the Victorian British garrison played cricket and hosted matches with visiting British Naval personnel. The game was embraced by the Corfiots and for many years the chalked impression of wickets and bails marked many an end wall in the squares of the Old Town where local youngsters played. Today, cricket on Corfu is an essential part of the summer scene on the Esplanade – or has been until recently. The pitch is currently closed and it is not yet known whether it will be restored. A touch rough and ready, it has produced a skilled breed of Corfiot fielders. Visiting clubs from England play regularly on the island, and the Corfu team has represented Greece in European Cup games.

Diving and the Law

The Greek authorities are extremely sensitive about security at military installations on the island. The use of underwater cameras is forbidden by law unless prior permission is obtained from port authorities. Divers are strongly advised not to dive in working harbours or at busy anchorages.

Basketball

Basketball is now almost as much of a national sport as football in Greece. On Corfu, in every resort, there will be some form of basketball practice area. Even private houses at the end of obscure tracks have net stands in their gardens or fixed to a side wall. There are basketball courts at the New Port in Corfu Town, where games can be watched.

Cricket

Cricket is a famous legacy of the Victorian British Protectorate. Matches are traditionally played on summer afternoons at the north end of the Esplanade, in front of the Liston (► panel, this page).

Kerkyra Cricket Committee
☎ (06610) 47754

Cycling

For information on cycling and mountain-biking (► 12–13).

Moraïtika Bike Hire
Rentals to suit all the family.
✉ At southern exit of Moraïtika

The Mountain Bike Shop
Rentals, cycling trips and holidays arranged.
✉ Main street, Dassiá
☎ summer (06610) 93344, off-season (06610) 97609. Also has a branch at Grecotel Dafnila Bay Thalosso Hotel, Dassia

Mountain Mania Bike Hire
In same office as Watermania, which arranges boat hire and excursions.
✉ Main street south, Sidári

Pink Panther Bike Hire
Rentals and trips arranged.
✉ Sidári, at the main Sidári/Roda intersection
☎ (06630) 95710

Diving

There are outstanding diving venues in the clear waters round Corfu's coasts. Although there is only minimal tidal movement to contend with in the Ionian, there are some dangerous currents, and winds can be fierce at times. Contact a local diving club or school for safety information (► panel this page for regulations).

Calypso Diving Centre
The centre is located right on the beach
✉ Ágios Gordis
☎ (06610) 53101

Cavos Diving Centre
✉ Main Street, Kávos

Corfu Divers
P.A.D.I. teaching centre offering openwater boat diving and all types of dives with instruction.
✉ Kassiopi ☎ (06630) 29226

Corfu Diving Centre
Runs boat trips to numerous excellent diving sites, for beginners to advanced. Lessons available for all abilities. Arranges specialist night dives and cave exploration.
✉ Paleokastritsa
☎ (06630) 41604

Ionian Divers
Runs courses and holidays for all abilities. Qualified instruction to British Sub-Aqua Club standard at all levels.
✉ Dassiá ☎ (06610) 90320

Golf

Corfu Golf Club
Corfu's only golf club has an 18-hole course in pleasant surroundings, with a winding river to add to the challenge. Described by *Encyclopedia of Golf* as 'one of the greatest courses in Europe'. Putting green, practice area and club professional.

✉ **Rópa Valley** ☎ **(06610) 94220/1** 💷 **Expensive**

Horse Riding
Horse riding is a pleasant and relaxed way of discovering the quieter side of Corfu, away from the beaches and popular resorts. Riding stables offer organised rides. The horses and ponies are well-trained and docile. Children who are capable of riding are catered for.

The Riders' Club
Horse and pony riding for the beginner and the experienced rider. Rides of approximately 1½ hours with picnic and transport provided.

✉ **Áno Korakiána** ☎ **(06630) 22503, 094 964332 (mobile)** 💷 **Moderate**

Rópa Valley Riding Stables
Horse and pony riding for the beginner and the experienced rider. Rides of approximately two hours, with a stop for refreshment.

✉ **Érmones** ☎ **(06610) 94220** 🕐 **Daily rides at 9:30AM and at 3PM** 💷 **Moderate**

Squash

Louis Corcyra Beach
The squash courts at this luxury hotel are available to non-residents by arrangement.

✉ **Gouviá** ☎ **(06610) 90196** 🕐 **Apr–Oct**

Tennis
Several luxury and A-class hotels have their own tennis courts which may be available to non-residents by arrangement.

Corfu Tennis Club
The club has four hard courts in a pleasant setting in Corfu Town.

✉ **4 Romanou Street/Vraila Street, Corfu Town** ☎ **(06610) 37021** 🕐 **The courts are available to non-members from 8AM to midday**

Ten-pin Bowling

Corfu Holiday Palace
The Corfu Holiday Palace has ten-pin bowling on its premises and the court is open to non-residents by arrangement.

✉ **2 Nafsikas, Kanóni** ☎ **(06610) 36540** 🕐 **All year**

Watersports
Most of the main resorts and several much smaller beach areas offer watersport facilities from pedaloes and canoes to banana boats, ringos, jet-ski trips and paragliding. Rental outfits operate from most beaches and beachside hotels have hire outlets and supervised watersport facilities which are usually available to non-residents.

Windsurfing
Windsurfing is an increasingly popular pastime on the breezier beaches of the west coast and at some suitable east coast resorts. These are good waters to learn on, to have fun on, or to enjoy speed sailing on, though there is not much scope for full-on wave jumping.

There are windsurfing centres at the following resorts: Ágios Geórgios (Northwest), Ágios Geórgios (Southwest), Ágios Górdis, Ágios Stéfanos (Northwest), Aryllas, Avlaki Beach, Érmones, Glyfáda, Kávos, Moraïtika and Sidári.

Nude Bathing
Officially, nude bathing is illegal in Greece, although some beaches are now designated officially as 'naturist'. Bathing nude 'unofficially' is best done with discretion. The Corfiots are broadminded but many will be offended by full nudity, especially near centres of population or within sight of a church. Topless bathing by women is virtually the norm on all beaches, but you should respect the sensibilities of local people when off the beach and near religious institutions.

General Photography
Photographs are among the best things to take home from Corfu and the opportunities for all types of photography are limitless. However, near military installations, and at other sensitive sites on Corfu, notices indicating that photography is forbidden should be heeded, or you may find yourself surrounded. In churches, monasteries and museums check first whether or not photography is permitted.

What's On When

Pot throwing

At 11AM on Holy Saturday morning the remarkable custom of pot throwing takes place. This involves large earthenware pots, sometimes filled with water, being dropped from windows and high balconies in Corfu Town. Pots are also smashed in villages. There are numerous explanations of this custom, ranging from it being a reference to Judas's betrayal of Christ for a pot of gold, to the joy of the Virgin Mary at discovering Christ's tomb to be empty, to its being a hangover from Venetian customs of throwing out old goods at the turn of the seasons, to prehistoric rituals of pottery breaking at burials. Whatever the explanation, stand clear...!

January

1 January – New Year's Day.
6 January – Epiphany. Religious ceremonies held.

February–March

Pre-Lenten Carnival. During the three weeks before the start of Lent, carnivals take place at various villages on Corfu. On the Sunday before Lent (seven Sundays before Easter) there is a big carnival procession in Corfu Town. Clean Monday, Kathari Deftera – the Monday after Carnival Sunday. Public holiday in Greece. On Corfu it is celebrated by families and friends going on huge picnics. Kite flying.
8 March – St Theodora's Day. The saint's remains are carried around Corfu Town.

April

Easter (movable). The most important celebration of the Greek year. A genuine re-birth. On Corfu, numerous religious services are held during the preceding Holy Week.
Palm Sunday – the remains of St Spyrídon are carried in procession through Corfu Town.
Good Friday – numerous church processions through Corfu Town and at villages.
Easter Saturday – procession from Church of St Spyrídon. Pot throwing custom (➤ panel this page). Atmospheric late evening candle-lit ceremony of the Resurrection on the Esplanade. Fireworks display.
Easter Sunday – Resurrection parades from churches in Corfu Town and villages. Countless fairs throughout the island.

May

1 May – national holiday festival at Róda and on Mount Ag Deka.
4 May – Feast of St Thomas festivals at Sidári, Gastoúri and Benítses, among others.
8 May – festival at Kassiópi.
21 May – Ionian Day. Anniversary of the Ionian Islands union with Greece in 1864. Local holiday. Procession in Corfu Town. Brass band display on the Esplanade.

June

Pentecost Sunday –festival at Lákones.
Whit Monday – festivals at Kondókali, Stavros and Argirádes, among others.
29 June – major festival celebrating St Gáios at Gáios on Paxos.

July

8 July – St Prokopios's Day. Festival at Lefkímmi.
26 July – St Paraskevi's Day. Festivals at Avliótes, Ágios Matthéos, Benítses, Ipsos, Kinopiastes.

August

6 August – Saviour's Day. During the preceding week there are pilgrimages to the summit of Mount Pandokrator (➤ 26). Festivals in Campiello district of Corfu Town, Ágios Matthéos and Strinýlas.
11 August – St Spyrídon's Day. Major procession of casket holding the saint's remains through Corfu Town.
15 August – Assumption of the Virgin. National holiday. Corfiots traditionally return to home villages. Festivals at Platitera Monastery (➤ 44) and at numerous villages.

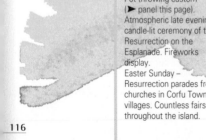

Practical Matters

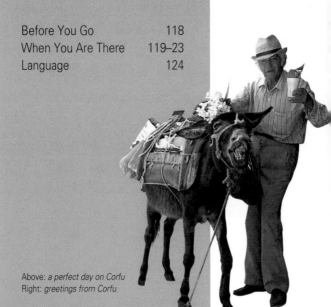

Above: *a perfect day on Corfu*
Right: *greetings from Corfu*

117

TIME DIFFERENCES

GMT
12 noon

Corfu
2PM

Germany
1PM

USA (NY)
7AM

Netherlands
1PM

Spain
1PM

BEFORE YOU GO

WHAT YOU NEED

	Required	Some countries require a passport to remain valid for	UK	Germany	USA	Netherlands	Spain
●	Required	a minimum period (usually at least six months)					
○	Suggested	beyond the date of entry – contact their consulate or					
▲	Not required	embassy or your travel agent for details.					
Passport/National Identity Card			●	●	●	●	●
Visa (Regulations can change – check before your journey)			▲	▲	▲	▲	▲
Onward or Return Ticket			▲	▲	▲	▲	▲
Health Inoculations (tetanus and polio)			○	○	○	○	○
Health Documentation (reciprocal agreement ▶ 123, Health)			●	●	▲	●	●
Travel Insurance			●	●	●	●	●
Driving Licence (National or International)			●	●	●	●	●
Car Insurance Certificate (if own car)			●	●	●	●	●
Car Registration Document (if own car)			●	●	●	●	●

WHEN TO GO

Corfu

High season

Low season

14°C	15°C	16°C	19°C	23°C	28°C	31°C	32°C	28°C	23°C	19°C	16°C
JAN	FEB	MAR	APR	MAY	JUN	JUL	AUG	SEP	OCT	NOV	DEC

 Very wet   Wet   Cloud   Sun   Sun/showers

POLICE	100
FIRE	199 FOREST FIRE 191
AMBULANCE	166
TOURIST POLICE	(0661) 30265

WHEN YOU ARE THERE

ARRIVING

Charter flights from European capitals go direct to Corfu in season. Olympic Airways operate flights daily from Athens to Corfu. Ferries run to Corfu from Ancona, Bari and Brindisi in Italy. Ferries run between Igoumenítsa on mainland Greece and Corfu. KTEL buses run twice daily between Athens and Corfu.

Corfu Airport	Journey Times	
Kilometres to Corfu Town		N/A
		N/A
2 kilometres		10 minutes

New Port Ferry Terminal	Journey times	
Kilometres to Corfu Town		N/A
		N/A
1.5 kilometres		5 minutes

MONEY

On January 1, 2002, Greece adopted the euro. Euro notes come in denominations of 500, 200, 100, 50, 20, 10 and 5; coins in denominations of 2 and 1 euros, 50, 20, 10, 5, 2 and one cents. Foreign currencies and travellers cheques can be exchanged at banks, bureaux de change and travel agents. Visa, Mastercard and Eurocard are widely accepted in the main resorts and can be used to take out cash from ATM machines at most banks.

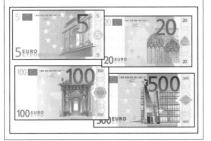

TIME

 Corfu, like the rest of Greece, is 2 hours ahead of British time. Greece puts its clocks forward 1 hour in summertime, around the same time as they change in Britain.

CUSTOMS

 YES
From another EU country for personal use (guidelines)
800 cigarettes
200 cigars
1 kilogram of tobacco
10 litres of spirits (over 22%)
20 litres of aperitifs
90 litres of wine, of which 60 litres can be sparkling wine
110 litres of beer

From a non-EU country for your personal use, the allowances are:
200 cigarettes OR
50 cigars OR
250 grams of tobacco
1 litre of spirits (over 22%)
2 litres of intermediary products (eg sherry) and sparkling wine
2 litres of still wine
50 grams of perfume
0.25 litres of eau de toilette
The value limit for goods is 240 euros

Travellers under 17 are not entitled to the tobacco and alcohol allowances.

 NO
Drugs, firearms, ammunition, offensive weapons, obscene material, unlicensed animals.

EMBASSIES AND CONSULATES

UK	Germany	USA	Netherlands	Spain
(0661) 30055 & 23457	(0661) 31453	(01) 721 2951 (Athens)	(0661) 39900	(0661) 39620

WHEN YOU ARE THERE

TOURIST OFFICES

Ellinikos Organismos Tourismou (EOT)

● (Greek National Tourist Organisation)
On corner of Rizopaston Voulefton and I. Polila streets
☎ (06610) 37520/36740
email: eotcorfu@otenet.gr
website: www.gnto.gr
🕐 8AM–2PM Mon–Fri

The offices in Corfu Town listed above are the main sources of tourist information. The Tourist Police are also important sources of information and are best referred to if visitors encounter difficulties with, or have complaints about, accommodation or service.

Most resorts have at least one private tourist agency. These organise a whole range of tourist services and will often be happy to give basic information, though it should be remembered that they are businesses. Leaflets on places of interest, car rentals and excursions can often be found at the reception desks of larger hotels.

EMAIL AND INTERNET

Corfu Town now has several internet cafés including K@fe On Line, Kapodistriou 28 (opposite the Esplanade) ☎ (06610) 46226 and Cyber Café Corfu, Gardikioti 3 (200m west of the new port ☎ (06610) 35384. A few of the larger resorts also have internet cafés, usually open until midnight or 1AM.

NATIONAL HOLIDAYS

J	F	M	A	M	J	J	A	S	O	N	D
2	(1)	1(2)	(1)	1	1		1		1		2

1 Jan	New Year's Day
6 Jan	Epiphany
End Feb/early Mar	Clean Monday
25 March	Independence Day
Mar/Apr	Good Friday and Easter
May 1	Labour Day
June 3	Holy Spirit Day
Aug 15	Feast of the Assumption
Oct 28	Óchi Day
25 Dec	Christmas Day
26 Dec	St Stephen's Day

August 11 the Feast of St Spyridon is an unofficial public holiday on Corfu. Shops and some restaurants close on public holidays. In Corfu Town and in main resorts, tavernas and most shops stay open.

OPENING HOURS

○ Shops	● Post Offices
● Offices	◐ Museums/Monuments
● Banks	◐ Pharmacies

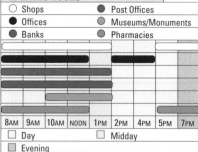

8AM 9AM 10AM NOON 1PM 2PM 4PM 5PM 7PM

☐ Day   ☐ Midday   ☐ Evening

In addition to the times in the chart above (which are given as a guide only), supermarkets and gift shops, particularly in resorts, often stay open until 9 or 10PM. Pharmacies are closed on Saturday and Sunday. Corfu Town post office is on Alexandras Avenue and opens Mon–Fri 7:30AM–8PM. Exchange bureaux are open until 10PM. It is always advisable to check the opening times of museums and sites locally as these vary from summer to winter.

DRIVE ON THE RIGHT

TOILETS Basic

PUBLIC TRANSPORT

 Internal Flights Domestic flights are operated by Olympic Airways (☎ 010 966 6666), and it is possible to make connections at Athens to Corfu. Olympic Airways domestic flight tickets are non-transferable. All Olympic Airways internal flights are non smoking.

 Island Buses Corfu's rural bus service is run by the national bus company, KTEL (Kratiko Tamio Ellinikon Leoforion). All services start from and return to Corfu Town. Timetables may be subject to change, but reliability is generally assured. Buses can be boarded anywhere along country roads, and tickets are purchased on board. KTEL buses also run between Corfu and Athens. The KTEL terminus in Corfu Town is at the northwest end of Avramiou. For information ☎ (06610) 30627.

 Ferries Ferries run between Corfu Town and Igoumenítsa on the mainland at half-hourly intervals in winter, and as frequently as 15-minute intervals in summer. Ferries also run at hourly intervals between Lefkímmi Port on the southern tip of the island and Igoumenítsa.
International ferries run between Bari and Brindisi in Italy and Patras on the Greek mainland, calling at Corfu Town. Ferry connections between Corfu and Paxos are uncertain and should be checked carefully through several agencies. Greek ferries move very quickly in and out of ports; always be ready to disembark as soon as the ramps touch the quay.

 Urban Transport Blue buses operate from San Rocco Square to the suburbs and Gastoúri (Achilleion), Kondokáli, Gouviá, Dassiá, Pérama, Benítses, Pélekas, Kanóni, and central Corfu. Pay on board or, for buses marked *horis eispraktor*, 'without conductor', buy tickets at the kiosk by the San Rocco bus rank.

CAR RENTAL

 Make sure you have Collision Damage Waiver. However, even with CDW you are liable for damage to tyres and undercarriage, so do not drive conventional vehicles off-road. The minimum rental age is from 21 to 25.

TAXIS

 Call radio cabs on (06610) 33811/2. Taxi ranks in Corfu Town are at San Rocco Square, the Esplanade and New Port. Meters should display the fare; if not determine cost beforehand. Double rates apply outside Corfu Town.

DRIVING

 Speed limit on national highways: **100kph**

 Speed limit on outside built-up areas: **80kph**

 Speed limit in built-up areas: **50kph**

 Must be worn in front seats and in the rear where fitted. Children under 10 years are not allowed in the front seat.

 80 micrograms of alcohol in 100ml of breath is a criminal offence, and from 50 to 80 micrograms a civil offence. There is random breath testing.

 Super, unleaded and diesel are all available. There are few petrol stations in rural areas and they tend to be the most expensive. They open daily (morning only) but may close on Sunday. Cash payment is preferred in rural stations. A useful word is *yemitse*: fill.

 It is compulsory to carry a first-aid kit, a fire extinguisher and a warning triangle. Tourists with proof of AA/RAC or similar membership are given free roadside assistance from ELPA, the Greek motoring club. If your vehicle breaks down, dial 104. There are good repair shops in big towns but in rural areas petrol stations can usually find a local mechanic.

CENTIMETRES

INCHES

PERSONAL SAFETY

Corfu is a safe island generally, but crime is on the increase, especially in crowded places. Report any problems to the Tourist Police, who can often speak several European languages.

- Leave money and valuables in hotel safe. Carry only what you need and keep it hidden.
- Women travelling alone can expect some minor harassment from *kamaki*, men on the lookout for a sexual encounter. Be firm in your refusal.
- Do not touch stray dogs. If bitten get medical help.

Tourist Police assistance:
☎ **(06610) 30265**
from any call box

TELEPHONES

The new 10-digit telephone system in Greece now means that for all calls within the country, whether local or long distance, the area code must be used. Furthermore, a '0' has been added to the end of each area code, hence what was (0661) 45678 is now (06610) 45678. Phone boxes take OTE phonecards, available from local shops and kiosks, and are the cheapest way to make international calls.

International Dialling Codes

From Corfu to:

UK:	00 44
Germany:	00 49
USA:	00 1

POST

Post Offices
Post offices are identified by a yellow 'ELPA' sign. Queues can be long and slow and if you only want stamps (*ghramatósima*) for postcards, try kiosks or shops selling cards. Normal post boxes are yellow, express boxes are red. Post offices are generally open Monday to Friday 8–2.

ELECTRICITY

The power supply in Greece is 220 volts AC, 50 Hz.

Sockets accept two-round-pin continental-style plugs. Visitors from the UK require a plug adaptor and US visitors will need a transformer for appliances operating on 100–120 volts.

TIPS/GRATUITIES

Yes ✓ No ✗		
Restaurants (service inc.)	✓	change
Cafés/Bar (if service not inc.)	✓	10%
Taxis	✓	change
Tour guides	✓	discretionary
Porters	✓	€1–2
Chambermaids	✓	discretionary
Hairdressers	✓	10%
Restroom attendants	✓	30 cents
Toilets	✗	

PHOTOGRAPHY

What to photograph: ancient sites (photography is free for hand held cameras) on most, villages, parades, harbours. The Greek people also like being photographed, but it is polite to ask permission.

Where you need permission to photograph: in some museums and always if using a tripod. Never photograph near military installations.

Where to buy film: the most popular brands are available in all tourist areas. The sunlight is brilliant in summer and it is a good idea to use a lens filter

HEALTH

Medical Treatment

Visitors from the European Union (EU) are entitled to reciprocal state medical care in Greece and should take with them a form E111 available from post offices. However, this covers treatment in only the most basic of hospitals and private medical insurance is advisable. British doctors and staff practice at: The British Surgery, Mantzarou 1, 49100, Corfu ☎ (06610) 49350 Fax: (06610) 49350

Dental Services

Dental treatment must be paid for by all visitors. Hotels can normally provide names of local English-speaking dentists; alternatively ask the Tourist Police. Private medical insurance is strongly advisable to cover dental treatment.

Sun Advice

Corfu enjoys sunshine for most of the year, and from May until September it is almost constant. During July and August, when the sun is at its hottest, a hat, strong-protection suncream and plenty of water are recommended. Try to keep out of the midday sun.

Drugs

Pharmacies (*farmakio*), indicated by a green cross sign, can give advice and prescriptions for common ailments. If you need prescription drugs, take the exact details from home. Most pharmacies have someone who can speak English.

Safe Water

Tap water is chlorinated and is regarded as safe to drink. Bottled water is is cheap to buy and is widely available. Drink plenty of water during hot weather.

CONCESSIONS

Students/Youths An International Student Identity Card (ISIC) can provide travel discounts and substantial reductions on entrance fees to museums and archaeological sites.

Senior Citizens Most museum and archaeological sites have reduced rates for elderly visitors. There are few other concessions but senior citizens can take advantage of the off-season rates in spring and October – ideal times to visit the island.

THE GREEK ALPHABET

The Greek alphabet cannot be transliterated into other languages in a straight-forward way. This can lead to variations in romanised spellings of Greek words and place-names. It also leads inevitably to inconsistencies, especially when comparing different guide books, leaflets and signs. However, the differences rarely make any name unrecognisable. The language looks complex, but it is worth memorising the alphabet to help with signs, destinations etc.

Alpha	Αα	short a, as in hat
Beta	Ββ	v sound
Gamma	Γγ	guttural g sound
Delta	Δδ	hard th, as in father
Epsilon	Εε	short e
Zita	Ζζ	z sound
Eta	Ηη	long e, as in feet
Theta	Θθ	soft th, as in think
Iota	Ιι	short i, as in hit
Kappa	Κκ	k sound
Lambda	Λλ	l sound
Mu	Μμ	m sound
Nu	Νν	n sound
Xi	Ξξ	x or ks sound
Omicron	Οο	short o, as in pot
Pi	Ππ	p sound
Rho	Ρρ	r sound
Sigma	Σσ	s sound
Tau	Ττ	t sound
Upsilon	Υυ	ee, or y as in funny
Phi	Φφ	f sound
Chi	Χχ	guttural ch, as in loch
Psi	Ψψ	ps, as in chops
Omega	Ωω	long o, as in bone

- The airport departure tax is added to the price of your ticket when you purchase it.
- It is forbidden to export antiquities and works of art found in Greece.
- Allowances for exporting other goods vary with the destination – check before departure.
- Confirm your flight times the day before departure.

LANGUAGE

The official language of Corfu is Greek. Many of the locals speak English, but a few words of Greek can be useful in rural areas where locals may know no English. It is also useful to know the Greek alphabet – particularly for reading street names and road signs (► 123). A few useful words and phrases are listed below, with phonetic transliterations and accents to show emphasis. More words and phrases can be found in the AA *Essential Greek Phrase Book*. Because the method of translating Greek place-names has changed recently, some spellings may differ from older ones you find on the island.

hotel	*xenodhohío*	toilet	*twaléta*
room	*dhomátyo*	bath	*bányo*
...single/double	*monó/dhipló*	shower	*doos*
for three people	*ya tría átoma*	hot water	*zestó neró*
can I see it?	*boró na to dho?*	balcony	*balkóni*
breakfast	*proinó*	campsite	*kamping*
guest house	*pansyón*	key	*klidhí*
toilet paper	*charti iyías*	towel	*petséta*

bank	*trápeza*	credit card	*pistotikí kárta*
exchange office	*ghrafío sinalágh-matos*	travellers' cheque	*taxidhyotikí epitayí*
post office	*tahidhromío*	passport	*dhiavatíryn*
money	*leftá*	can I pay by...	*boró na plíróso me...*
cash desk	*tamío*		
how much	*póso káni*	cheap/expensive	*ftinós/akrivós*
exchange rate	*isotimía*		

restaurant	*estiatório*	bread	*psomi*
café	*kafenío*	water	*nero*
menu	*menóo*	wine	*krasi*
lunch	*yévma*	coffee	*kafés*
dinner	*dhípno*	fruit	*fróoto*
dessert	*epidhórpyo*	waitress	*servitóra*
waiter	*garsóni*	tea (black)	*tsái*
the bill	*loghariazmós*		

aeroplane	*aeropláno*	...single/return	*apló/ metepistrofís*
airport	*aerodhrómio*		
bus	*leoforío*	car	*aftokínito*
...station	*stathmós*	taxi	*taxí*
...stop	*stási*	the road to...	*o dhrómos ya*
boat	*karávi*	no smoking	*mi kapnízondes*
...port/harbour	*limáni*	timetable	*dhromolóyo*
ticket	*isitírio*	petrol	*venzíni*

yes	*né*	goodbye	*....adío* or *yásas, yásoo*
no	*óhi*		
please	*parakaló*	sorry	*signómi*
thank you	*efharistó*	how much?	*póso káni?*
hello	*yásas, yásoo*	where is...?	*poú eené..?*
good morning	*kalí méra*	help!	*voíthia!*
good evening	*kalí spéra*	my name is...	*meh léne*
good night	*kalí níkhta*	I don't speak Greek	*then miló hellliniká*
I don't understand	*katalavéno*	excuse me	*me sinchoríte*

INDEX

Acknowledgements

The Automobile Assocation wishes to thank the following photographers, libraries and associations for their assistance in the preparation of this book:

AKG LONDON 10b, 11b; MIKE GERRARD 33; DES HANNIGAN 8b, 12b, 31a, 39, 42b, 47a, 60b, 91b INTERNATIONAL PHOTOBANK 21b; MUNICIPAL ART GALLERY, CORFU TOWN 34; PICTURES COLOUR LIBRARY 1, 8c, SPECTRUM COLOUR LIBRARY 50b, 71; TRAVEL INK 77b (Brian Hoffman), WORLD PICTURES LTD 2, 6/7, 58, 67b, 73; www.euro.ecb.int 119 (euro notes).

The remaining photographs are held in the Association's own photo library (AA PHOTO LIBRARY) and were taken by Steve Outram with the exception of the following: Pete Bennett F/cover (d) sunbather; T L Carlsen 13c; Steve Day F/cover (a) Greek flag, B/cover dinghy, 122b; Philip Enticknap F/cover (b) flowers; Terry Harris 5b, 63b, 63c; Ken Paterson F/cover (h) coffee, F/cover bottom squid, 13b, 52b, 62c, 91a, 92, 93, 94, 95, 96, 97, 98, 99, 100, 101, 102, 103, 104, 105, 106, 107, 108, 109, 110, 111, 112, 113, 114, 115, 116; Jean François Pin F/cover (c) windsurfer; Anthony Sattin 80b, 81b, 83b; J A Tims F/cover (g) belfry, 5a, 6a, 7a, 8a, 9a, 9d, 10a, 11a, 12a, 13a, 14a, 14b, 18b, 23c, 26b, 27a, 31b, 37b, 46/7, 49b, 57b, 65b, 72b, 76b, 79, 117b; Martin Trelawny 9c, 17b, 27b, 43b, 53a; Peter Wilson 62b.

Des Hannigan wishes to thank friends and associates in Corfu for their assistance. Special thanks to Stacey Flanagan and Bryan Jones, Hilary Whitton Paipeti, Maria and Noofris Michalakis, Susan Daltas, and Alex Kritikas.

Copy editor: Rebecca Snelling Revision management: Outcrop Publishing Services, Cumbria

Dear Essential Traveller

Your comments, opinions and recommendations are very important to us. So please help us to improve our travel guides by taking a few minutes to complete this simple questionnaire.

You do not need a stamp (unless posted outside the UK). If you do not want to cut this page from your guide, then photocopy it or write your answers on a plain sheet of paper.

Send to: **The Editor, AA World Travel Guides, FREEPOST SCE 4598, Basingstoke RG21 4GY.**

Your recommendations...

We always encourage readers' recommendations for restaurants, nightlife or shopping – if your recommendation is used in the next edition of the guide, we will send you a *FREE* AA *Essential* **Guide** of your choice. Please state below the establishment name, location and your reasons for recommending it.

_____

_____

_____

_____

Please send me **AA *Essential*** _____

(see list of titles inside the front cover)

About this guide...

Which title did you buy?

AA *Essential* _____

Where did you buy it? _____

When? m m / y y

Why did you choose an AA *Essential* Guide? _____

_____

_____

_____

_____

Did this guide meet your expectations?

Exceeded ☐ Met all ☐ Met most ☐ Fell below ☐

Please give your reasons _____

_____

_____

_____

continued on next page...

Were there any aspects of this guide that you particularly liked? _____

_____

_____

_____

Is there anything we could have done better? _____

_____

_____

_____

_____

About you...

Name (*Mr/Mrs/Ms*) _____

  Address _____

_____

_____ Postcode _____

  Daytime tel nos _____

Which age group are you in?

  Under 25 ☐ 25–34 ☐ 35–44 ☐ 45–54 ☐ 55–64 ☐ 65+ ☐

How many trips do you make a year?

  Less than one ☐ One ☐ Two ☐ Three or more ☐

Are you an AA member? Yes ☐ No ☐

About your trip...

When did you book? m m / y y   When did you travel? m m / y y

How long did you stay? _____

Was it for business or leisure? _____

Did you buy any other travel guides for your trip?

  If yes, which ones? _____

_____

Thank you for taking the time to complete this questionnaire. Please send
it to us as soon as possible, and remember, you do not need a stamp
(*unless posted outside the UK*).

Happy Holidays!